WHEN CANADA DREAMED

PRAISE FOR PREVIOUS BOOKS BY SEAN KANE

Wisdom of the Mythtellers

"This could be the most important book published in Canada in 1994." – *Canadian Book Review Annual*

"The book establishes Sean Kane as an important successor to Northrop Frye. Provocative and compelling, this is a book to be savoured and debated." – *Literary Review of Canada*

"This volume is a humanist's approach to myth, implicitly drawing on literature, art, history, archaeology and zoology. This confluence makes for delightful reading. It is a gracefully written book, a pleasure to read and absorb." – *Journal of American Folklore*

"A rare and wonderful introduction to mythic thought [that] marks an advance in relating this human activity to our entire relationship with the Earth and the world we live in." – Robert Lawlor, author of *Voices of the First Day: Awakening in the Aboriginal Dreamtime*

Virtual Freedom

"Uproarious send-ups of our stagnant liberal arts campuses. There is plenty of wild farce, of loony but lovable characters and delicious digressions." – *The Globe and Mail*

"*Virtual Freedom* presents a hilarious intellectual Eden just after the Original Sin of turning education into a business. Sean Kane populates his weedy garden with dead-on caricatures and lovable rebels whose real fight is with themselves. It should be required reading for those brave souls considering the at once absurd and worthy enterprise of a B.A. in our increasingly literalist age." – Andrew Pyper, international bestselling author

Raccoon: A Wondertale

"*Raccoon* will be recognized as a classic of its genre. It joins all those currents of thought that see the creative imagination as the ultimate force that can reshape and somehow, in some way, redeem the planet." – Eugene Benson, emeritus professor of English, University of Guelph, and co-editor of the *Encyclopedia of Post-Colonial Literature*

"This account of an ideal Commonwealth is in the tradition of some of the finest adventure stories ever written. Sean Kane's clear-eyed, beautifully written tale offers a critique of society as it is, and a model of what it could be." – Stan Dragland, emeritus professor of Canadian and Children's Literature, Western University

"*Raccoon* is an extraordinary work of fiction. Alive with incident, madcap excitement, quirky humour, and many poetic turns of phrase, it is at once a satire, a wondertale, and a thoughtful work of ecological commentary." – Don LePan, founder and CEO of Broadview Press

"How can we live without Sean Kane's inspired madness? His loopy intelligence, and the amplitude of his heart, provide necessary medicine for all creatures working for a collective swerve away from ecological catastrophe and finding themselves wounded by the battle." – David Abram, Senior Visiting Scholar in Philosophy and Social Ecology, Harvard University

"*Raccoon* feels real and has bite. It has Sean Kane's – but how does he do it? – grasp of where the imaginative and real meet. Everything in his story sparkles with that and because of that." – Gordon Teskey, Francis Lee Higginson Professor of English Literature, Harvard University

The mind supplies the idea of a nation,
but what gives this idea its sentimental force
is a community of dreams.
ANDRÉ MALRAUX

WHEN CANADA DREAMED
*Growing up in the absurd world of Canadian writing
and publishing in the Age of Great National Dreams*

Sean Kane

Rock's Mills Press
Rock's Mills, Ontario • Oakville, Ontario
2025

The names in this book are real, the characters fictitious.

Published by
Rock's Mills Press
www.rocksmillspress.com

Copyright © 2025 by Sean Kane.
All rights reserved. No part of this publication may be reproduced, distributed, or transmitted in any form or by any means, including photocopying, recording, or other electronic or mechanical methods, without the prior written permission of the publisher, except in the case of brief quotations embodied in critical reviews and certain other noncommercial uses permitted by copyright law. For permission requests, contact the publisher at customer.service@rocksmillspress.com.

For information about trade, library, and bulk orders, please contact the publisher at customer.service@rocksmillspress.com or through our website.

*For Owen and Natasha Kane
and for Ainsley Inessa Kane*

DREAMS AND REFLECTIONS

What not to do with time | 1

1. Canada's National Publisher | 3

Briefly a mother | 10

2. The Hero | 15

Who will speak for wonder? | 39

3. Wonder | 41

The worldspin | 54

4. The Open Road | 56

How couples met | 73

5. First Love | 75

A between time | 86

6. Becoming a Writer | 89

A sacred trust | 106

7. Medicare | 112

Literary studies today | 119

8. The Liberal Arts College | 121

Cause-besotted generations | 132

9. A National Literature | 134

10. Prophet to a Nation | 148

What's to be done with the past? | 164

11. The Critic | 167

12. Survival | 178

13. Mastery | 188

The legacy of the old | 199

14. Dying | 202

Three minutes in Paradise | 212

15. Heaven | 214

16. Friendship | 223

Notes | 237

About the Author | 249

Image Credits | 250

WHEN CANADA DREAMED

What not to do with time

Riiiiiiiiiiiiing! Riiiiiiiiiiiing!...

"Hi!"

"Good time to talk?"

"We'll have to keep it short."

"Just checking in. What's new at your end?"

"Oh ... not much. Tash is working at Markham General today. I'm working on my Shakespeare paper."

"When's that conference? I forgot."

"In three weeks. Any publishing news?"

"Nothing exciting. I'm waiting for Peggy to tweet *Raccoon*. Then the fur will fly. Otherwise, it's under the radar."

"It'll sell slowly ... just a sec."

WHRRRRRRRRRRRRRRRRRRRRRRR!!!

"Ouch! Can you hold the phone away from the coffee grinder?"

Silence.

"Sorry. Where were we?"

"You said it'll sell slowly. I suppose that's because..."

HIIISSSSSSSSSSSSS!

Silence.

"Okay, I'm back. Just pouring it into the thermos...There! I meant sales are probably on par for a literary press. The book's not being picked for review because it wasn't good enough to publish commercially."

However accurate, the assessments of the young leave something to be desired. Yet they are a compass to guide me in this mean, abrupt time.

Sound of something metal hitting a hollow wall. Muffled laughter.

"Are you listening…?"
"Yes, I'm here. I was just talking to a neighbour."
"You're taking your bike down the elevator?"
Muffled exchange. Laughter.
"Okay, I'm back."
"I was saying…"
Traffic noises. A car horn.
"Can you hear me? Where are you anyway?"
"I'm on my bike. I'm late for work."
"Look, let's talk later. Call me tonight?"
"Deal."

Reference points: I am the father on the phone. I am old and getting older by the minute and I've just published a work of fiction. Listen to me: Don't do this! Don't ever do this. Here is the wisdom of an elder. Old age is not for the faint-hearted. Commercial publishing is not for the faint-hearted either. Not to mention the further challenge of trying to keep up with a son determined to carve out a future in a world in chaos. At the moment, he's bicycling through rush-hour traffic to work in an athletics store. I'm sure he's going to be hit by a car and break his collarbone. Whatever income he makes from selling sports equipment will be augmented by contract teaching. Academic for hire. Maybe his partner will fix his collarbone.

Time moves at different velocities for the young and the old. The young consume it to fuel a career – multi-tasking exploits several time streams at once. The old have "time on their hands."

Stupidly I have used it to write a literary novel.

A father leaving the stage. A son coming onstage. Unknown decades separate us. I'll pass on the dreams of my generation, for what they're worth. It is time for me to say goodbye to them anyway.

I
THE DREAM OF CANADA'S NATIONAL PUBLISHER

I can't remember a time when I wasn't surrounded by books. My earliest childhood memory is being read to by my aunt, a children's librarian, and thinking that the people inside the book were using her mouth so they could be heard. Books were everywhere in the house – in the kitchen, the bathroom, the corridor, the stairway. And not just books but loose, stacked pages on their way to becoming books. The manuscripts were sandwiched between cardboard stiffeners which the hand laundry at the corner inserted in my father's shirts to make them presentable. I cut the shirt cardboards up with scissors to make forts and castles held together by cellotape. Television wasn't allowed in the house. My father was a book publisher and knew by instinct that visual culture was a threat to the fun of reading. Not to mention the fun of publishing.

Trade publishing came with the smell of cigarettes, Bloody Marys, and late night phone calls, this one at 4 a.m.:

"... It's confirmed: she's still in the water!"

"What about the other two?"

"One of them cramped out. The other was hauled out shaking. I guess she didn't like eels sucking on her."

"Eels? Jesuschrist! Where are you getting this from?"

"From Ron. He's got a direct line to a spy in the coaching boat."

It is 1954, and a seventeen-year-old high-school girl at Loretto Abbey in Toronto is attempting to be the first woman to swim across Lake Ontario. Florence Chadwick, the conqueror of the Catalina Strait, has been hauled out vomiting. Winnie Roach, who mastered the English Channel, is cramping in the 21°C water and is finished. But little Marilyn Bell is plunging on against fifteen foot high waves. She says she's "doing it for Canada." Will she make it? A nation's reputation hangs in the balance. Even more important, so does a book about Marilyn's brief history in long-distance swimming by sports writer Ron McAllister, which in anticipation of the historic event is already written except for the triumphant final chapter. (Mr. McAllister would arrange for me to sit next to Foster Hewitt in the play-by-play broadcast gondola high over Maple Leaf Gardens, to watch a Detroit-Toronto game.)

Gentlemen's publishing was knowing how to bet on the winner in wanton disregard of the concept of budgeting for profit. Jack McClelland, the voice of the late-night phone calls that punctuated my childhood, turned down the account of another heroic journey made by a Labrador Retriever, a Bull Terrier, and a Siamese cat. The three lost buddies travelled 480 kilometres across the northern Ontario wilderness, protecting each other from bears and wolves, to find their way home to their owner, the author Sheila Burnford. "It'll never sell," Jack decided. *The Incredible Journey* sold 200,000 copies in the U.S. and was made into a film twice by Walt Disney.

"She's fighting an offshore current and a crosswind, but I think the gal's going to make it."

"Where are we with production?"

"I told them to start typesetting."

Marilyn Bell reached the shoreline near the Canadian National Exhibition at 8:15 that morning, welcomed by crowds of people drawn by hourly updates on the city's radio stations. She'd been in the water 20 hours and 59 minutes. The media frenzy lasted for weeks. *Swim to Glory! The Story of Marilyn Bell and the Lakeshore Swimming Club* reached the bookstores just before Canada's national darling appeared on *The Ed Sullivan Show*, prime-time network TV in America.

"We had the goddam book in print before the gal was halfway across the lake," the publishers boasted.

Hugh Kane, starting out
(Hugh Kane Archives)

My childhood was punctuated by heroic adventures which were turned into books. A year earlier, Sir Edmund Hillary and Tenzing Norgay reached the top of Mount Everest, becoming the first recorded climbers to conquer the highest mountain in the world. I heroically climbed the Himalaya of book cartons stacked twelve feet high in the McClelland and Stewart stock room, scaling the crevasses, careful not to start an avalanche. The books filled 20,800 square feet of shipping and storage space. Canadian publishing was never so aspiring, nor so precarious.

But animals made better heroes, as far as Canadian book publishing was concerned. I helped choose the jacket image for *Beautiful*

Joe, the story of a loyal dog who paid the price. Poor Joe's ears had been mutilated by some unkind person, so he was pictured with his ears in a bloody head scarf heroically leaping a fence. Dog sagas were marketed for children who were grieving the loss of a pet and needed to understand the meaning of a short, passionately loyal life. You knew from page one of the book that the dog was going down. My father was soft on sacrificial animal tales. He owned successively two Cocker Spaniels and a Beagle who greeted him enthusiastically when he came home to Summerhill Gardens from work. When he died, he was buried with a Milkbone in his suit pocket. Jack, who was inclined to asthma, may not have been so sentimental about animals, especially the succession of McClelland family Afghan hounds, including the one who ran away from home daily, stopping to pee on Ira Berg's shop window at Yonge and St. Clair before reaching the Summerhill Park where it was sent home in a taxi. Both colleagues shared the opinion that Canadian authors generally wrote better about animals than about human beings. This view was confirmed by Farley Mowat who when asked about his faith said, "I probably believe in God the same way my dog does." His *The Dog Who Wouldn't Be* was a prize-winning children's book. Farley's pooch sat wearing goggles in the open back seat of a roadster rumbling across the Prairies, eating cherries and spitting the pits into the wind. After its publication, countless dogs were named "Farley." At the age of fifteen, attending the Canadian Librarian's Association Conference, I was scooped up by Mowat and taken to a deep-sea salvage tug in the harbour of Quebec City to be introduced to Newfoundland Screech. Farley deposited my senseless corpse on the hall carpet outside by father's hotel room in the Chateau Frontenac and fled for his life.

Jack McClelland and Hugh Kane became a team at McClelland & Stewart when they returned from World War Two, Hugh to marketing and promotion, Jack to assume the presidency of the firm from his father. They got along because they shared a wicked sense of humour and because each recognized that the other was driven. Hugh served on the boards of several of the legendary New York publishing houses, representing their authors in Canada through the M&S sales networks he cultivated. In his youth he had gone to New York to learn how to be an actor. He never made it to the stage; instead he picked up the romance of the Manhattan literary scene – Dorothy Parker and the Algonquin Round Table, the great literary editor Maxwell Perkins, the publisher Alfred A. Knopf. Jack came out of a family background in agency publishing, but his heart lay in working personally with authors and promoting their writing. Hugh and Jack's partnership is told in memos written with a hilarious tragic joy as they try to locate a business compass lost in the day's excitement. For no matter how heroically they worked, they couldn't make a profit publishing trade books for the

Jack McClelland
(Courtesy of Anne McClelland/McMaster University)

Hugh Kane
(Hugh Kane Archives)

small Canadian market. Nobody could in those days. The memos often ended in affectionate scolding curses. Overhearing my father pour his exasperation into a device called a Dictaphone, I never understood what the sign-off letters G.F.Y.! meant. I thought they meant Good for You. Teetering financially at its glorious sunset, McClelland & Stewart had a staff of eighty. Jack tried to turn the ship around by betting on media personalities, franchise authors, and high-risk ventures. Hugh, whose principle was to publish the book not the author, later found the ease to publish what he thought best as president of Macmillan of Canada, which balanced educational and trade publishing. He published Dennis Lee's *Alligator Pie* children's nonsense verse, emerging poets like Gwendolyn MacEwan, and the eminent Canadian novelists Hugh MacLennan, Morley Callahan, and Robertson Davies, as well as well-known historians and politicians. But even this balance didn't hold. Head office in London was concerned. Hugh came home muttering to his spaniel, "Budget for profit. What the hell is that?"

Yet between them Jack McClelland and Hugh Kane published most of the great writers of classic Canadian literature, coaxing them along with heartfelt letters and unforgettable launching parties. From 1951, when they ousted their superiors at McClelland & Stewart, to 1972 when Hugh, now at Macmillan, conspired with Jack to unite the two rival companies to fulfill their dream of one big, solvent Canadian-owned publisher, they worked together. Both died from the delayed effects of strokes that waited for them — Jack at age 74, Hugh at 73 — two Total Publishing Dawgs driven by passion, loyalty, and self-sacrifice.

Briefly a mother

MY MOTHER HAUNTS MY DREAMS like a whimsically curious ghost. How am I going to introduce her when I recall so little? She played intricate Bach fugues on her piano while I snuggled behind it among huge post-Pre-Raphaelite canvasses, my hiding place. The movers had to hoist the piano on a handmade crane with pulleys, then ease it lengthwise through an opening they made by removing an entire window. It cost a bundle to do, but the piano saved her life. She was dying of boredom. She used the day to bake bread which she put on the hot water radiators to rise. She read contemporary novels. She taught Sunday School at St. Paul's United on Avenue Road. She hung out with her personal and as far as I can tell only best friend, Herta, an Austrian woman with a dachshund. She wrote cryptic poems in elegant artistic letters in the margins of her hymn book. When she felt like it, she made dinner. The quirks of a grown-up seen through a child's eyes.

And she laughed at the smallest absurdity and couldn't control the laughter because it recycled the incident in her mind so that just when she thought she'd stopped laughing, that itself was funny and she laughed some more. I inherited her laughter in utero. At night, she played double solitaire with my father. I'd hear her cry of triumph when she slammed a card down on the card table a second before him. She played Bach on the piano, he played "Danny Boy." She was a long way from home.

Her home was the West Coast. She had spent her childhood in the 1920s Vancouver bohemian sub-culture, with artists like Emily Carr travelling up Island or into the Rockies to paint. Her father, John Day, born in Salisbury, was an art dealer from New York

Dorothy Kane and Herta
Buchberger of the Old Vienna
Book Shop on Avenue Road

where he made a success buying up late nineteenth-century European paintings that had dropped in value because of Abstract Expressionism but were treasured by nostalgic immigrants. Judging from the works behind the piano that escaped my father's purge when he remarried, John Day had an eye for the Japanese colour woodcut – an artistic trend in the period of Gilbert and Sullivan's *The Mikado*. The colour woodcut master Urishibaru influenced a young English craft artist newly come to Canada by the name of Walter J. Phillips, who reproduced the Ontario wilderness, Winnipeg streets, and ultimately the Rocky Mountains in the thick outline and delicate balance of art nouveau.

It takes a patient artist to make a woodcut and print it in one colour, then hang the sheets up to dry and work on a second colour for the same composition, then a third, then a fourth. I count nine separate colours in "Mamalilicoola" in my living room. In the circumstances of slow, painstaking composition, Walter Phillips needed a sponsor, and John Day served as both patron and art dealer for his prints. While in Winnipeg, Phillips was known to Charlie Pyper and to Nancy Pyper – I write the married couple's names separately because they had distinct public careers. C.B. Pyper was a journalist, made famous by his reporting of the Spanish Civil War and for inserting himself on the Royal Train and drinking across Canada with George VI and Elizabeth on their crucial tour before the outbreak of the Second World War. Nancy was a celebrity actress who crashed the lives of Irish notables from W.B. Yeats to Bernard Shaw whose plays she performed in, first in Winnipeg, then in Toronto where she hosted a regular soirée while managing the Hart House theatre. At the fall of France in 1940, she entered the soirée naked and draped in the tricolour like the painting of Liberté, performing what was known at the time as an attitude and declaiming, "Alas, poor France!" My aunt Alice Kane found her ridiculous for saying things like "dahrling!" but for a young Hugh Kane, his aunt Nancy and uncle Charlie brought him close to what was hot in Toronto culture. The celebrity couple even had a sundae named after them in a Bloor Street restaurant. To make a long story short, Nancy and Charlie invited John Day to their soirée attended by Hugh. Day brought with him a shy, sensitive daughter called Dorothy who had the vulnerability and need for protection that appealed to men at the time. This was 1938. They married immediately.

Whatever Hugh was like before the War, he came back changed and worldly. Serving in the army of occupation in Wilhelmshaven, he brought home a complete German-made electric train set in his knapsack. But I had become changed and worldly too in my three short years in the company of my grandfather, a gruff former seaman. When my father tiptoed into my grandfather's Montreal house in the middle of the night, he was greeted by a wide-awake child sitting at the top of the staircase. The child said: "Who the hell are you?" In contrast to my father, my mother was otherworldy. She had the air of being orphaned. I have only a small sense of her mother, Tedina Craig or "Teddy," who was an actress in West Coast theatre. It is enough to make me think the daughter took refuge in solitude. Hilary Mantel has written about the silencing effect of a powerful parent on a child: "Unwanted or superfluous children have difficulty in being embodied; they remain airy, available to fate, as if no one had signed them out of the soul store." Aunt Alice told me in a memoir: "Make no mistake about it: you had a good mother, and your ability to write and speak and communicate was given to you by her. You were read to, recited to, played with, and above all talked to." But all I can remember is leaning out of the gable window with my mother and chanting:

> *I hear leaves drinking rain.*
> *I hear rich leaves on top*
> *Giving the poor beneath*
> *Drop after drop.*

Alice also recalls periods of anxiety when my mother couldn't cope with the responsibilities put upon her – often a sign of depression. Yet Dorothy had her own bright personality when her husband wasn't around. The Christmas party at her mental care home was a costume dance. West Coast people love the frivolity of costume parties; she dressed up as a fetching, bare-armed, long-haired Indigenous princess. Dancing with her doctor, she held her tomahawk just over his head.

Though not suicidal, she may have known she carried her early death within her. Every so often something drops out of one of her books, like this verse typed on thin fragile paper:

It was strange oh Fawn, to thee
Thy rapid race of life
'Tis done.
No more the rains upon thee fall —
No more the sun.
  Yet death was quick —
  It had to be.
  For did it not catch
  Up to thee?
Each breeze, each forest song, each tree —
  Shall rustle on
  Unheard by thee.
But life goes on —
Through endless, endless years
Men shall laugh o'er the
Heap of your grave —
Shall shed no tears —
  I who must remember —
  I who saw thee fall.
  Will die sometime — like you —
Oh, Fawn —
    Will be forgot by all.
                    – Dorothy Day

Faint impressions, but they linger to tell a story.

2
THE DREAM OF THE HERO

Crescent School, now we sing of thy glory!
Long may you serve as you have in the past;
Honour and Truth are a part of your story;
May they grow in our lives to the last!
Onward ever, we will serve thee,
Faithful to the Green and Grey.
Proudly, we march up the future's broad highway,
True to all people and School for aye!

The School Song sounds in my head whenever I receive a bright mailing from Crescent. Today, the institution is located in the upper Bayview area of Toronto, not on the city's eastern outskirts where it was when I knew it, and it serves a globalised meritocracy instead of old Toronto wealth. Yet its mission of instilling ethical values in future leaders is still going strong. That mission is signalled in the mailing by the phrase *Great Boys*.

What's so great about Great Boys? I guess alumni with money to donate will instantly recognize themselves in the phrase. But in case they don't, here's the Headmaster advising that the School is developing "a new strategic plan." The mission of "building character" in boys will now be extended to Athletics, Performing Arts, Robotics, and Outreach. "Therefore, the ideal Crescent graduate – a Man of Character – will be principled, wise, resilient, and engaged."

The Headmaster doesn't use the word, but it seems the bedrock of character is still what used to be called *Virtue*. "However, current research clearly demonstrates that there are three other important character domains: intellectual, performance and relational." Intellectual character requires knowledge and judgment. Performance character is persistence in achieving a goal. Relational character involves "those habits of engagement through which one offers one's best self in service to the broader community." Moral character, intellectual character, performance character, relational character. Haven't we met those four virtues before?

Let's go back to Alexander the Great, surely the most precocious Great Boy of all. That was partly because his tutor was Aristotle. One imagines the young Alexander, dreaming of future empires bigger than his father's, asking his teacher to name the one outstanding virtue needed to achieve his dream:

"Use current research, and give me a strategic plan by nightfall."

"*Megalopsychia*," said Aristotle promptly.

"What's that?"

"It is an aspiration to achieve honour."

"How, precisely?"

"By doing public-spirited acts that have the effect of displaying 'magnificence' (*megaloprepia*)."

"Libraries! I shall build a public library in every city! People will read about your ideas."

And so the teacher's idea of the big-hearted, public-spirited citizen was stamped on his student Alexander, who would stride the world, creating individual city-states complete with grandiose libraries. In the early twentieth century, the American steel magnate Andrew Carnegie demonstrated his greatness of soul by endowing a public library in every small city in North America, and you can recognize them today by their Corinthian pillars. Carnegie displayed his big-heartedness in spite of his attitude to the Amalgamated Association of Iron and Steel Workers. But we shouldn't expect such ostentation in our Men of Character today. They're more suited to the down-to-earth Roman version of public virtue, known as magnanimity.

Enter Cicero. He was aware of the need to train an elite of colonial administrators for a Republic that suddenly found it had an empire. A colonial administrator was likely to be a military officer. Accordingly, Cicero equates greatness of heart with stoic courage. He sees courage as having four parts. One of them is *magnificence* – "the consideration and putting into action (*administratio*) of great and lofty matters with a certain greatness of soul and noble purpose." It looks like magnanimity has sunk from its place as the crowning virtue: it's now a self-conscious promotional style by which a public figure demonstrates their breadth of character. In the delirium inspired by a new strategic plan talking about moral virtue in today's investors, I hear those old Roman values reasserting themselves. If the Crescent Man of Character is "principled, wise, resilient, and engaged," is he not displaying the four classical virtues: Temperance, Wisdom, Courage and Justice? Temperance (moral character) is discerning the right conduct and matching it to society's norms. Wisdom (intellectual character) is the sober second thought that comes with experience. Courage (performance character) is setting the right goals and sticking to them under stress. Justice (relational character) is discerning a fair relationship between people in a community. Enough of this casuistry – let's just say it: Greatness of soul means not being a twit.

In the Crescent I knew, still honouring the traditions of empire, becoming educated was a heroic process. Education for empire was vivid in the saying I saw later at Upper Canada College across the top of Mr. Galloway's Geography class blackboard:

> *Ride hard,*
> *Shoot clean,*
> *Fear God,*
> *and Honour the Queen.*

This mission statement in red, white, and blue chalk remained unerased by the night cleaners. It had remained unerased since the Boer War of 1899 to 1902 when the saying and probably Mr. Galloway originated. We think of heroism as belonging to the extraordinary individual: someone we can erect a statue to. But Crescent taught me that heroism really belongs to a community. The hero is the *pro tem* challenge-taker who steps forward and accepts a risk on behalf of the others. When he triumphs, the whole community is stronger. Why? Because the risk-taker extends the range of experience the community feels it is capable of. In this way, boys advance in a group into the future in small existential leaps.

This heroism worked out of sight of teachers and their absurd notions of character-building. Small communities of boys aged 5 to 14 automatically produced the right leader for the occasion. In contrast, the School's official leadership training framework – a competitive sports program, extracurricular activities, and "broadening" educational opportunities – produced a hierarchy of "prefects" lording it over inferiors. The system alienated the ones with imagination and sidelined those who lacked athletic prowess. Going on at Crescent, out of the sight of teachers and their appointed twits, was a community of heroes keen to make a contract with the future where none of them had gone before.

"I dare you," someone said to Dick Starr, "to go out the window, cross the roof, and come back in the far window." This was a worthy dare. The dormitory room roof had slate shingles you could slip on; it was three stories above the ground; and the boys couldn't get to sleep until they had proved something to themselves. They proved through their proxy that sheer nerve could triumph over fear of heights. For this particular challenge, Starr was their *pro tem* leader. Other leaders would emerge as needed to expand the envelope of achievement according to their respective skills.

There's no photograph of him from this period, except a group shot of the senior hockey team, and this portrait doesn't represent him accurately because Starr was not a team player. For that reason, he was placed in goal. We could rely on his height and composure to defend the crease, which he would do so long as no one told him what to do. In his relaxed taciturnity punctuated by a mischievous wit, he combined the gifts of his parents. His father, Ukrainian-Canadian, was the sort of handsome serviceman who was chosen to be photographed for the war effort, with the camera tilted upwards to catch a face looking bravely into the distance. His mother, a war bride, came from the Anglo-Italian population that gave London the Rosettis and much of Bloomsbury. Stature and eloquence united in Richard Derek Starr.

Yes, you could turn down a dare. Realistic judgment was valued in a leader. There was an ecology of achievable dares, and by judiciously accepting or turning them down leaders re-set the calibration on what could and couldn't be accomplished in the life of a community. But no aspiring hero could continually reject a dare without dropping a rung in the community's esteem. Starr took the dare for the basic reason that he considered it was doable – so long as he didn't start to shake.

Twelve, then twenty, then a host of boys summoned from nearby dormitory rooms watched Starr crawl out the south window in his pajamas. They waited in awe for him to go splat on the terrace below. The moon peeked out of clouds to witness the deed for herself. Eventually, after an excruciating interval, we heard a scratching at the north window. Everyone tiptoed across the floor in their bare feet. Starr re-entered to great acclaim. That acclaim echoes in my ears a lifetime later. I trust it still echoes in his.

It took me a while to understand that the hero isn't necessarily and probably shouldn't be the centre of power in a heroic community – a principle which takes the whole of the *Iliad* to work out. There needs to be a separation of powers between Agamemnon and Achilles, between Charlemagne and Roland, between a U.S. president and the Pentagon. At Crescent, the week's current events were posted on a large newsprint sheet attached to a stand. It mentioned something called an atomic bomb that could make a city go poof, and a general called Douglas MacArthur who was a twit because

The school from the north

he wanted to drop one of them on China. Nothing on these news sheets told us how to be a hero. We worked out how to be men of character ourselves in the forty acres of landscaped parkland that surrounded the main building.

Crescent in its Arcadian heyday was hand-picked to be the setting for a heroic culture. The 100-room mansion built by Walter Edward Hart Massey in 1913 offered a curving grand staircase, a carpeted reception room, an arboretum, a gentleman's library, a swimming pool, and a theatre designed for a young Raymond Massey, who would go on to become a Hollywood actor. When classes were over at 4:00 and the Day Boys had departed, the borders exploded in a mass of anarchic energy onto the school grounds. Parents who had read *The Prospectus of Crescent School* may have thought their children were enjoying "Ample facilities for nature study and walks and general outdoor life" in the "Forty acres of meadows, woodland, and three large playing fields." In fact, kids were at the intersections of make-believe worlds.

I can't write of this setting without being wistful. The original

Massey estate house which became the Upper School was built on a plateau that rose in the middle of a system of streams. Visitors ascended it from the west, following a winding drive that took them over a bridge between two large ponds. They would notice a blur of golden-orange in the water – a school of carp. Weeping willow trees surrounding the ponds. In the distance, on the other side of a creek, was a playing field. It could be reached from the School by a path with cement stairs and terraces that went down the hillside. In every detail, the approach to the estate house was designed to be an event.

At its eastern edge, the plateau dropped off in a wooded hillside traversed by landscaped paths. The forest paths once conveyed a large Edwardian family and servants in elegant procession to a patio with statues overlooking the Rose Garden, where they would take tea. The formal paths were augmented over the years by an interlace of secret trails taking boys to hideouts. Here, on the hillsides around the Rose Garden with its Pre-Raphaelite Wishing Well, we spent most of our free time when the weather was good. Adjacent to the Rose Garden was another playing field. Along its far side was the northern creek. Behind the eastern goal posts was a wire fence with a slanted barbed-wire top which every Crescent boy learned to scale by the age of seven, to explore a swamp outside School property.

Walkway from the School to the western playing field

To the north, the plateau ended abruptly in a cliff overlooking a large vegetable garden gone to ruin – the Massey family manufactured tractors for the Canadian Prairies, and they operated part of the property as an experimental farm. Here the northern creek ran through sandy soil with willows. This area was dangerous and consequently out-of-bounds, which gave it even more allure.

On the south side, the plateau sent out a spur at the end of which was a stable with two bored horses for Saturday horseback riding. Below the plateau, a southern stream fed the carp ponds. In a financial crisis, the headmaster of Crescent in 1958 ceded this area to the Township of Scarborough to use as a garbage dump. This polluted the ponds instantly. The ancestral carp went belly-up, adding to the stink of scandal greeting every visitor to the School. Fleeing lawsuits, the headmaster was said to have traded in the school car at Ted Davey's Used Car Lot on the Danforth, and that was the end of Arcadia.

In an age before computer games, children grouped together spontaneously to create their own world to play in. If they were boys, their imaginative realms were influenced by adventure storybooks, war movies, and cowboy westerns. These various worlds overlapped according to the mutual acceptance of make-believe. There were no rules – except this one: when the housemaster on duty blew his whistle, boys had to stop whatever they were doing and assemble around him. A roll call would be made to ensure no one was hurt or missing, then the boys were set loose again until the final whistle called them in for dinner and homework. Supervision was light; people were less anxious about child safety in those days. Young people were left alone to choose leaders for themselves, never to be forgotten. I recount those names now: Assaf, Pickles, Chalk, Tibley. And the inimitable Dick Starr.

Approaching Christmas Break, there were outbursts of festivity on the dormitory floor. Soon, we would be home with our parents.

"Deck the halls with Assaf's balls," bellowed Starr. "Fa-la-la-la. La-la-la-la-la!"

Billy Assaf celebrated Christmas at a later time. I have a memory of him attending the Syrian Orthodox Church, probably the longest-running Christian community. What made Assaf a singularity was his urge to re-create the dynastic grandeur of biblical film epics like *Spartacus*. Earlier in the fall, he had organized a gang of boys from the junior grades clutching spears made from reeds plucked from the forbidden swamp. These minions were over-awed by the sight of Assaf the Great carried on his throne platform by four slaves stripped naked to the waist, and fanned by two boys holding ferns.

We were apprised of these details by a spy planted in the cedar copse above Assaf's fort in the Rose Garden. It was vital to know how far advanced his defenses were. Any day, he might raid our fort for slaves.

Our fort, hidden in the pines behind the Rose Garden soccer field, was built to withstand a protracted siege. Like the combined war bands of the Athenian Confederacy in the time of the Persian invasion, we were fewer in number than Assaf's army, but we had a technological superiority. The key to that superiority was a fabulous artificer who outshone the legendary Daedalus of Crete. He was named Chalk. Now Chalk must surely have become an engineer in later life because during his time at Crescent he did nothing but dig tunnels and build forts. This he did with a singleminded public-spiritedness that irritated the gods. In the early autumn, he dug a network of tunnels in the hillside below the riding paddock. It took a group of teachers a whole afternoon to collapse it. Then Chalk took to digging a hole near the Wishing Well. Because he was a person of few words, we could only anticipate the hole was going to be enlarged at the bottom to create a club house. Yet there was no sign of this happening as Chalk in his tireless lonely industry kept digging straight down trying to reach China. From 4:00 p.m. when we were let out until the final whistle calling us in, Chalk was in his hole, selflessly constructing something magnificent for the common good. Such was the genius we employed to build our fort. Chalk found cedar logs from a farmer's split-rail fence outside the property and made a pioneer's log cabin. For insulation, he stuck plugs of turf between the beams. For the roof, he found flat boards which he wove together using willow branches. The structure was impregnable to the new military technology that was threatening to take gang warfare to a new level. This was the slingshot. Made from wire coat-hangers and industrial-strength elastic bands and firing pebbles, it made the horses grazing in the paddock rise in the air and gallop in snorting circles. When the teachers noticed pebbles inexplicably embedded in the bark of trees, an investigation took place and the weapon was banned.

Assaf sent a raiding party to capture one of our younger members. His name was Tibley. He was taken to Assaf's fort and tied to a tree. Soon after, an emissary appeared outside our fort, waving his white school handkerchief on a spear. The emissary, as I recall, was Philpot – a provoking name to have at a boys' school were it not for the fact that his uncle was one of the three heroes who escaped from Stalag Luft III by means of the stratagem of the Wooden Horse. We knew this from a recent movie.

"If you want to see Tibley alive, you must pay tribute to Assaf the Omnipotent…"

"Get lost, Philpot."

"The tribute shall be turf cut in neat squares. Moreover, you are commanded to deliver the aforesaid tribute on your knees, bowing to his Omnipotence upon approaching his solemn presence."

"Tell Assaf to disappear up his rectum."

"Oh, and you have to put Double Bubble gum on top of the tribute," Philpot added, breaking into the vernacular. "We know you've got it because we found some on Tibley."

Small pink rectangles wrapped in coloured comic strips, the gum was banned at Crescent. Having become the basis of a system of currency, it led to theft and endless dispute.

"Set Tibs free, or you all die," we replied.

The emissary departed. The cavalry saddled up for war.

To become the U.S. Cavalry, boys took their school belts out of the loops of their pants and wore them on the outside of their jackets. School handkerchiefs encircled the neck like bandanas. Thus transformed, they would gallop in to save the day, just like the endings of twelve-cent Saturday matinee westerns at the Alhambra Theatre. The gallop they affected might have been a fair pretense at riding a horse at full speed, if they didn't have to hold their pants up with one hand. The intention was to ride into the centre of Assaf's imperial court, shoot the place up, and free Tibley, who was now tied by his hands to a tree branch with his feet just touching the ground in a simulation of torture.

"I've been thinking," said Pickles. "We don't want Tibley back. We want Assaf obliterated. Otherwise, he's going to become an even bigger asshole."

"There aren't enough of us," Starr reckoned. "He'll see us coming and fall back on his fort. He probably has spies watching us right now."

The shifting role of leader sometimes settles briefly on the one who gives wise counsel. Thus it settled on Odysseus, master of stratagems, in the combined Achaean army led by Agamemnon. "I have an idea," I said. "Let's give Assaf a tribute he can't even imagine. We'll hide our weapons in it and lay it at his feet."

"Cool!"

"Then, when someone gives the signal, we'll go for our weapons and drive Assaf's bodyguard back into the bushes."

"Free Tibley."

"Then the cavalry rides in and levels the place."

Chalk was about to speak. You could tell he was going to speak because he was excited. Chalk was rarely excited. "An idea for the tribute. Bulrushes. They're just at the right height in the swamp now. Plus turpentine oil from the paint shop to dip them in. They'll make great torches."

"Assaf will love it! He can make his slaves hold torches."

And that was how Assaf the Mighty was taken by surprise on

that historic autumn afternoon. We carried the tribute in, bowing to him while he sat on his throne, surrounded by slaves fanning him with ferns. We laid the tribute on the ground while we were searched by his lieutenants. No spears, no slingshots. The bulrushes were explained. They were accepted.

"Now!" said Starr.

We dove for our weapons, kicking the bulrushes apart to find them. Assaf's bodyguard retreated into the forest under a hail of stones and missiles. With his obsessive sense of public duty, Chalk began methodically dismantling the packing crates and fence logs of Assaf's fort. Holding their pants up with one hand, their spears with another, the cavalry rode in right on cue and forced Assaf's junior cohort to run for their lives. Assaf's bodyguard was fighting back now. It was going to be a brawl.

Tibley was smiling like an idiot on his tree, knowing that nothing bad would happen to him because everything that was going on was make-believe.

Then the housemaster blew his whistle.

Weapons were dropped. Everyone ran in a throng counting off the 180 seconds before Detentions were awarded. Panting, we gathered around the housemaster.

"Assaf."

"Here."

"Chalk."

"Here."

The list went on. Long before it got to the letter T, a tragic realization dawned on the boys one by one.

"Tibley."

"?"

"Where's Tibley?"

"..."

"Alright. Somebody tell me where Tibley is or the whole lot of you gets a Detention."

Finally, one of Assaf's slaves spoke up. "Sir, he's hanging from a tree, sir."

Tibley isn't his real name, of course. I don't remember what the sacrificial victim's real name was. Tibley is the appellation I'm giving to the type of personality essential to a community of great boys. That type is the Innocent Follower. He is the one who makes leaders possible and in some mute inglorious way takes on the greatness of the heroic community. The poet Carl Sandburg writes of him:

> *I am an ancient reluctant conscript.*
>
> *On the soup wagons of Xerxes I was a cleaner of pans.*
>
> *On the march of Miltiades' phalanx, I had a haft and head;*
> *I had a bristling gleaming spear-handle.*

The Innocent Follower takes a solemn pride in the ordinary task he performs for a community. So it was in the heroic culture of Crescent School.

After the Tibley incident, constant supervision of the borders was called for, and Mr. Niblock the housemaster made the job interesting while indulging his physical prowess. He engaged the boys in athletics. A new appointee, he wore the first track suit we had ever seen, and with his dashing lock of hair falling down and his moustache he might have stepped out of the 1936 Berlin Olympics. Everything about Percival Niblock was dashing. Running on the spot with his knees rising up smartly to an exaggerated height, he informed us that we were about to go on a cross-country run. Off we went, the whole population of borders stretched out behind in a straggling line, Niblock imposing his authority by means of blasts on his whistle. Down to the ponds, then upstream along the northern creek to the Rose Garden soccer field, then past the ruins of the Assaf Empire, up the wooded slope beyond Chalk's legendary tunnels – Niblock blowing his whistle continuously like a nervous steam locomotive calling its train of freight cars. It took us some time to catch up to him at the stables, where we found him staring at a high bar he had previously erected for jumping.

"Regulation high jump. I will demonstrate the Scissors Kick. Following that, the Western Roll, which has recently replaced the Scissors Kick at most high jump competitions. You will see that there is a noticeable gain in height with the Western Roll."

Mr. Niblock walked about twenty paces away, removed his whistle, took deep breaths, focused his intensity, and after an explosive run sailed over the bar on his back, making a vigorous kick with his legs in mid-flight.

"The man is a zit," observed Starr.

Then, Niblock ran at the bar a second time, executing a Western Roll, coming to an elegant three-point landing in the pit on his outstretched fingers and one foot, the other leg extended horizontally backward.

Billy Assaf had the trace of a smile on his lips. It was the sardonic smile of one who believes the universe is ultimately a just place, and people get what they deserve. Having earned this wisdom in continuous Detentions over the last three weekends, he winked conspiratorially at Starr as if to say: "This guy is about to meet his Fate."

When the boys attempted the jump, the results were lamentable. Niblock, who clearly had a hyperactivity disorder, lost interest. He noticed a large fungus on the base of a tree. "A discus!" he cried. "Boys – back in your places. I will demonstrate the Discus Throw. The technique for successfully throwing the discus hasn't changed in twenty-four hundred years."

Our places were in a semi-circle around Niblock, arranged oldest to youngest, sitting with straight backs, legs crossed, hands folded in our laps. The position seemed to suit Tibley in his anonymity in the middle of the arc. No one's back was straighter as he sat in wide-eyed adulation of Mister Niblock. Tibley also believed in a just universe, but unlike Assaf whose belief was deeply warped, Tibley's belief was wide-eyed and innocent. For Mr. Niblock had become, in Tibley's eyes, a demi-god. And now this Herakles was going to demonstrate a technique that went back to the first Hellenic games on the plain beneath Mount Olympus!

"First, one winds oneself up, so to speak." Niblock slowly rotated his body, relaxed, then counter-rotated against the centrifugal trajectory of the planned release. He was coiled up like a spring, a crouching mass of potential energy, one hand on his bent knee, the other cradling a hard, yellow fungus. "Whereupon you explode your kinetic force along the trajectory of the throw, like *this*."

Percival Niblock spun like a whirling dervish. His throwing arm shot out in a Nazi salute. Forty pairs of eyes followed the flight of the fungus.

No discus could be seen. Niblocks's arm was still outstretched, yet the fungus had vanished. He pulled his lock of hair out of his eyes and squinted into the distance. He had felt the object leave his hand. Where was it?

"Holy shit!"

Tibley had fallen over backward. His legs were still crossed and his hands were folded in his lap. With his straight back, he resembled a toppled over Buddha, staring at the sky with a huge yellow fungus embedded in his mouth.

Niblock knew enough not to try to extract the fungus and the bits of teeth. He simply scooped Tibley up in his arms and with the exaggerated knee-high trot with which he began the afternoon took off along the gravel drive.

Tibley subsequently returned to the school and showed us his new teeth. Mr. Niblock was never seen again.

⋆ ⋆ ⋆

"*Hmmm* ... Teeth ... Hair ... Hands, Shoes ... *hmm* ... Stockings, Face, Handkerchief. Very good. Next boy."

The Headmaster checked off the seven attributes of a tidy appearance, always in the same order, while the boy being inspected stood at the front of a line-up of borders who had just swished their teeth with water, combed their hair once with their fingers, rubbed yesterday's ink stains off their hands, polished their black Oxfords, pulled up their stockings, splashed their faces with water, and arranged a clean white handkerchief in the breast pocket of their Harris tweed jacket. Each item was awarded a "1" in the Headmaster's great black-leather ledger with its red corners. Each boy accordingly started the day with seven credits, like poker chips, plus another three Neatness marks and three more for Punctuality. Most important of all, the Headmaster daily awarded four Good Conduct marks. Neatness and Punctuality were small stuff; lose a critical number of Conduct marks in a week and you would have a Weekend Detention and not get to see your parents. One could lose four or even eight marks at a time, depending on the mood of a teacher, who would theatrically record the deduction in a pocket notebook like a football referee issuing a yellow card. The ledger ruled our lives as if in anticipation of the book of the saved and the damned kept by St. Peter, who must surely be the patron saint of administrators. The moral calculus ruled us mentally and physically, until the night Starr broke its spell by an act of *ledgerdemain*. He altered his marks with the help of a flashlight.

Checking the deportment of each boy, the Headmaster hummed, translating tedium into a kind of intoned ritual which the boys found soothing. He had been humming, by all accounts, since 1930, when he took over the original school in Rosedale, bringing it three years later to Dentonia Park, the residence and estate donated by the Massey family. W. R. E. Williams (M. A. Cambridge) had served as

Teeth, hair, hands, shoes, stockings,
face, handkerchief

a commissioned officer in the Great War and subsequently joined the Military Staff College. Coming from a distinguished academic family, he had progressive ideas about the theory and practice of teaching and had studied Education at McGill. Because of his Welsh Methodist background – Williams had attended Oswestry School in Staffordshire and married a woman from Bristol – he was free of the upper-class Anglicanism that made the principal of Upper Canada College at the time an alien pomposity. Indeed, Mr. Williams seemed naturally friendly. He genuinely respected boys, and I can attest that while the word "pervert" was much in use by us for objectionable people generally, he was not one. There was, rarely, corporal punishment, for while this was a boys' school on the British model, punishment by Mr. Williams was a source of mirth because he hummed lyrically even while he was applying the official Board of Education strap to the hands. But he was becoming forgetful due to the effect on his arteries of the English cooking served by the school cook whose taste buds had been shot off at the Somme in 1916. Day-to-day management of the School was delegated to Mr. Carroll. A country veterinarian, he had discovered in the Royal Air Force that power accrues to the subordinate who does the accounting, and Mr. Williams with his ledger respected accounting.

Most of the academic staff came and went too quickly. Some were Australians putting in some fun in Toronto while they circled the globe. They taught us hearty, incomprehensible songs about a camper who waltzed with Matilda and a happy bird called Kookaburra who chewed gum in a tree. One teacher who stands out is Mr. Hopkins. With his permanent suntan, horn-rimmed glasses, and air of keenness, he was our first example of an American personality, in contrast to the post-war frumpiness of the Britishers. Mark Hopkins was probably from California because he bore the name of a famous San Francisco hotel and because he used the Religious Knowledge class to engage us in that West Coast fascination – Zen Buddhism. Hopkins succeeded in getting twenty boys in full lotus positions breathing with the cosmos before he mysteriously vanished. I don't remember the old-timers who resembled a row of gargoyles at the front of morning assembly. They started to disappear after Mr. Carroll consolidated his power by marrying the School Matron, thereby gaining a permanent apartment in Dentonia House, across the driveway from the school. I remember Mr. Clifton, who had a law degree from Osgoode Hall. He taught us the term *ecology* twenty years before it became a household word, and had us constructing retaining walls to preserve the eroding hillsides of the Rose Garden. And there was the ancient Miss Liston who presided over the Junior School. Formerly of Bishop Otter College, Oxford University,

Trinity College of Music, and the Royal Academy of Art, she was a woman of commanding professional poise, until the afternoon of her dismissal when in front of some one hundred boys queueing for taxis she screamed at Mr. Carroll: "You're nothing but a horse doctor."

As these glimpses show, Crescent offered its students lessons in the proper conduct of life. However, moral lessons are quickly assimilated into current social styles and in the late Fifties British form lost out to American individualism in the imaginations of young boys. Things English seemed quaintly peculiar, like the silly *Carry On* movies, and would continue to do so until English culture produced James Bond. When confined to "Sick Bay" with chickenpox, our reading material was boys' adventure books by G. A. Henty and English boys' magazines with photographs of cricket stars, steam locomotives, and HMS *Hood*. Our dormitory rooms, originally servants' quarters, were named for places having British military significance: *Croydon*, *Plymouth*, *Bay of Biscay*, and so on. Against this British background, we started to deploy a rebel outsider style. Our idea of a hero became the individual on whom everybody depends but who depends on no one. This aloof masculinity suited Dick Starr.

Now, I must recall for you a world of eight- or ten- or twelve-year-old boys in a state of being alone. I'm not speaking of the Day Boys. They tended to come from established Toronto families with lots of brothers and sisters and cousins, Osler Bluffs in the winter, Muskoka in the summer. Their parents sent them to Crescent for the educational and social advantages the School offered. But when they were whisked away in taxis at 4 o'clock, Crescent became a different place. The institutional hum given voice by the Headmaster, the noise that held us to a ritually organized schedule, died away, and when the lights were turned out at night forty boys were face-to-face with the reasons why they'd been sent to Crescent.

They were here because their families were dysfunctional. Their parents were unable to do the basic tasks of parenting. Or unwilling. They might be separated or divorced. They might be alcoholic. They might be workaholic. They might be single. Dick Starr was at Crescent on a Veterans Affairs Educational Scholarship – his father had been shot down in a Stirling bomber during the war. I expect my father outsourced parenting to Crescent because it took a burden off my mother. For most of my time at Crescent, I was a Day Boy; I became a border during the periods when she was hospitalized. The School was located between the new East York office of McClelland & Stewart Publishers and the Whitby Mental Hospital. My father would test children's book cover designs on a focus group comprising my peers, then drive me along the new MacDonald-Cartier Highway to the institution where women who seemed not at all insane crowded to the windows to admire Dorothy's boy in his cute school uniform.

At night, we were really alone. It got cold after the heating system was shut off. Those of us who couldn't sleep read comic books by flashlight or listened to country music from Wheeling, West Virginia, on muted radios. Sometimes, late at night, a boy would cry for no reason. Around dawn, the steam

Mother and son at the Well
in the Rose Garden

radiators began to make tormented clanging noises – the furnace had been turned on. It was on a night like this, with rain spattering on the dormer windows, and Starr in a foul mood because he had been singled out by Carroll for Detention, that he and I, sole residents of a small dormitory room called *Northampton*, remembered the boarded-up opening to a crawl-space behind the dormitory wall.

It was about the year of publication of *The Magician's Nephew* by C.S Lewis. Had we known that book then, we would have been prepared for what we discovered:

> The dark place was like a long tunnel with a brick wall on one side and a sloping roof on the other. In the roof there were little chunks of light between the slates. There was no floor in this tunnel. You had to step from rafter to rafter, and between them there was only plaster. If you stepped on this you would find yourself falling through the ceiling of the room below.

Beer bottles and pages of a newspaper left when the mansion was built evoked the notion of ghosts, and Starr, once he had measured off the distance to a particular dormitory, decided he would become one. I went back to *Northampton* to contemplate the mayhem that about to ensue.

Tibley. Is that you sleeping there? Wake up, Tibley.
"What? Who is it?"
"Sssh! Go to sleep, Tibley."
"No, you guys. Listen!"
Tibley. It's me. The ghost behind the wall.
"Jesus shit!"
Yes, Tibley. I'm the Ghost in the Wall. I'm coming to get You.
"Help! Ghosts in the wall!"
"Shut up, Tibley. There's nothing in the wall."
"No, there are ghosts. Listen."
You're right, Tibley. There's more of us here, came Starr's tremulous

voice. He imitated Vincent Price in the movie *Dracula*. *All coming to get youuuuu.*

Tibley shot out the dormitory door. "Run for your lives! There are Ghosts in the wall!" he screamed.

All coming to get you-u-u-u-u, Starr repeated in a quavering hysterical voice. It emptied the dormitory.

Everybody quiet down. I don't want to have to come over and give Detentions. This was Mr. Carroll on the intercom. I started the countdown on the stopwatch borrowed from the Athletics locker. Scrambling back up the tunnel, Starr also counted down two minutes. That was the time it took the housemaster to race across the main drive from Dentonia House and reach the dormitory.

Boys came streaming out of every room. Obedient to an emergency, some had gotten dressed and were holding their flashlights for a Fire Evacuation. All were convinced there were ghosts in the wall of *Tipperary*. And they were multiplying. The beams of flashlights criss-crossed. A flight of boys heading for the grand staircase to the Dining Hall met a group huddled in fear at the door of *Liverpool*. In *Croydon*, Chalk was dutifully stacking beds to form a barricade against ghosts.

"Ghosts," screamed Tibley. "They're after me."

The shout was taken up by the other boys. No one had thought to turn on the corridor lights.

Starr appeared and slipped into bed and was immediately asleep.

Carroll arrived out-of-breath. He turned on the lights. Boys were running in opposite directions up and down the corridor. Some were hiding in the bathroom — surely ghosts don't use the can. Several boys were outside the building, standing in the rain in the courtyard. Here was a boy with terror in his eyes, opening and closing his mouth like a goldfish.

"What's the matter? Why aren't you in bed?"

"It's Tibley, sir. He can't speak. He's afraid of the ghosts. But they aren't real. I'm not afraid, sir, though I do wish they would go away."

"Tibley. Come here. Now what's the problem?"

"Oh, sir. There are ghosts…" he wailed.

"Where are those ghosts?"

"Sir, they're in the wall. They're coming to get me."

"Listen, Tibley. Look at me. Look into my eyes. There. are. no. ghosts. in. the. wall. Got that? You were having a nightmare."

But Tibley wasn't buying this. The ghosts knew his name. A sleepy looking Dick Starr surveyed the chaos from the door of *Northampton*. It would take an hour to assemble the boys and calm them down. Then it would be another hour before anybody got to sleep. It would be sufficient merely to whisper the word *ghosts* and the turmoil would begin again. Carroll would have to spend the rest of the night on a spare bed in the dormitory corridor. Mr. Carroll was in a foul mood. Unlike Starr who now felt released from his.

These things happened in the time of Chalk and Assaf, and Dick Starr, tamer of passions. They do not reflect on the present Crescent School which from its alumni magazine seems a quite reasonable place.

The Prospectus of Crescent School assured parents in an age anxious about diseases of the lung that "The School's situation is known to be healthful; it is high and well above the point of condensation from Lake Ontario. The air is clear and bracing." Nonetheless, in the fall and spring, we used to have the most enchanting mists. Boys would race in and out of sight, disappearing into a spirit world. In 1956, my last spring at Crescent, as if to mourn Headmaster Walter Williams's recent death, the School and its grounds were shrouded in a fog. Starr and I took the opportunity to slip unnoticed over the barbed-wire fence with the swamp beyond and experiment with cigarettes.

Magically, as we penetrated the *terra incognita* beyond the school boundary, we encountered three of the aliens called "girls." About our age, 13, or maybe a little older, they stood staring at us. We stared at them. They'd been wading in the creek looking for frogs and were muddy. Their hair was lanky and stringy in the damp mist. The tallest one was their leader. Exhibiting a maturity that challenged the imagination, she had the most disarming freckles. Her complexion made us think of the Red River cereal in milk that awaited us at breakfast on Thursdays. In the silence, one of the girls expertly blew a pink bubble. We watched in awe as it got bigger and bigger, then popped without the gum plastering her face.

According to some ancient code, the freckle-faced leader produced packages of the bubble gum. We produced our cigarettes. The gifts were traded and immediately pocketed. We exchanged silences. Then, on an invisible signal, the girls turned and filed back into the mist like members of a lost Amazon tribe. We turned and walked back to the fence, thoughtfully.

"I bet she has freckles on her bum," Starr mused, introducing a new concept.

"Go back and ask her. I dare you."

Starr considered the idea. "It's better to leave some things to the imagination," he said.

I wasn't sure what to make of this remark, but we knew a chapter in our lives was over and we were about to cross into the future.

Who will speak for wonder?

Every so often the world of commercial advertising has a fling with wonder. Winged fairies and wide-eyed children are employed to link a feeling of exceeded expectation to a product. The results are laughable. The slogan, "We put the wonder back in air travel" crashed at takeoff. A biscuit said to have a "wonderfilling" lasted a little longer, probably on the strength of "Wonder Bread" which came to Earth around the time of the Roswell alien landing and is still with us. Then there is the TV ad of the wonderchild with ringlets who continually has to visit the loo. The moppet must have a bladder infection. But no – she skips upstairs to press a roll of toilet paper against her cheek to experience its velvety softness. A dreamy purple mist flows from the product to the girl's cheek.

Frustrated with why wonder doesn't work in the media, one advertiser struck back. An ad that ran during the Christmas shopping season pictured a little girl enchanted with a familiar object – the snow men inside a transparent plastic case. When she shook it, she magically created snow flurries. Her father comes along. "See the little snowmen?" he barks. "They're trapped just like Mommy and Daddy in their expensive data plan." He grabs the snow world and throws it on the floor, muttering "Freedom Mobile offers 100 extra Gigs." Daddy destroys a state of imagination – for what? A hundred extra Gigs.

How can wonder survive in a world of high-speed decision-making and staying ahead of the curve? It might be argued that it already does. Don't today's feats of engineering and technology produce wonders? The Burj Khalifa in Dubai and Saudi Arabia's Jedda Tower deserve to be added to the Seven Wonders of the World. But notice these are man-made constructions; wonder doesn't seem the right word for the products of human ingenuity. *Awe* or *marvel* are better for these glamours. My point is that wonder — a wary, affectionate openness to the strange — is diminished by explanation: if you explain a mystery, you explain it away. This distinction frees a very old word to draw on its ancient sense of something downward and covered, something *under*, belonging to Earth. Wonders, unlike the miracles of science, serve no end or purpose. Wonder is what philosophers call an "aesthetic emotion." You can't do anything with it — it just is!

But that doesn't mean wonder is without agency. Myths and folktales from around the world join wonder to a spirit of autonomy. "Now Ivon Tortik didn't know much," says a story from Brittany, "but what he knew was close to the ground. And one thing he knew was that fairy gold melts in the pockets of mortal men." So he told the fairies, "No, make me handsome." And that is how Ivon the hunchback got a straight back and married Margarride, the Miller's daughter.

Ivon in his soft fascination with the wonders in nature is different from the heroes of history at Crescent School and Troy. He travels with a high heart along the open road seeking his fortune. His adversaries are stuck in one place and perform some monotonous repetitive task connected with hoarding wealth. Like the troll with one eye of Norwegian folk tradition, they do only one thing, and they do it well. And so the age-old principle of conflict in storytelling: Wonder, without goals and free to wander. Control, driven by a shortsighted goal and stuck in one place.

3
THE DREAM OF WONDER

In times past there lived a king and queen who said to each other every day of their lives, "Would that we had a child!" yet they had not. But it happened once when the queen went bathing that a frog came out of the water and squatted on the ground beside her and said, "O Queen, your wish has been fulfilled. Before a year has gone by, you will have a child."

I don't recall my childhood all that well, but I still hear her voice clearly. Sometimes I think she put me in a spell of enchantment to insulate me from the indifferent parenting of her brother. He had never known male parenting: his father had been away at sea during his early childhood, and his in turn – the town doctor of Larne in Ireland – died young. But my aunt was a first-born daughter and close to her father. A children's librarian, she knew everything about boys and girls – their names, their favourite reading, their homework projects, their pets, the customs of their country of origin, everything. As for me, I grew up in a fairy tale setting: a remote and powerful father; an otherworldly mother; a child left alone in the world to seek their fortune. When I was ten years old, my mother died. Not long afterwards, I acquired a stepmother. But my fairy aunt had long since stepped in to fill the void.

Not just her, but her sisterhood of children's librarians. For she was just one of four women who babysat me. There was Miss Kelly who knew Taoist stories in Chinese and taught me how to paddle a canoe in Algonquin Park, Miss Armstrong who told of the Norse gods and took me to swim with her nieces and nephews in Georgian Bay, Miss Stedman, heiress to a chain of retail stores, who taught me shrewd folktales and how to handle money. They had been handpicked by Lillian H. Smith to serve in her Boys and Girls Division of the Toronto Public Library – chosen, it was rumoured, because they were brilliant, enjoyed children and as if by a solemn vow made to Miss Smith chose to exist beyond the reach of men.

Lillian Helena Smith (1887–1983) was a force in the creation of special libraries for children in the early twentieth century. She joined the Children's Department just started in the New York Public Library by the legendary Anne Carroll Moore. Miss Smith's own Boys and Girls House, once a large Edwardian home at St. George and College in Toronto, copied Moore's idea of a Central Children's Room where librarians specially trained to work with children learned to do puppet shows and storytelling. This was the mission Lillian Smith brought to Toronto in 1921: use the imaginative power of spoken stories to lead children to books so they can create worlds on their own.

Alice Kane and grand-nephew Owen

The special libraries for children were founded during the magical first decade of the twentieth century when people believed in wonder, and so the stories the librarians told came from the collections of fairy tales, hero stories, myths, and fantasy popular at the time. According to Miss Smith's regimen, the staff members chose the stories they would tell in the coming term from those traditional sources. They distinguished the best story from its known versions and defended their choice before all the children's librarians assembled at Boys and Girls House. They practiced the story in the mornings before the children came in. Moreover, each librarian had to be an expert in a genre of oral narrative. My aunt's specialty was the wondertale – "those longish fairy tales that have elements in them sometimes of myth, at other times of simple folktale, and always of enchantment." After her retirement, she became a performing artist in this genre, enjoying an international reputation and an honorary D.Litt. I don't think it's been recognized that Lillian Smith rescued children from their parents by giving them a magical realm complete with storytelling sibyls. These omniscient fairies produced just the right book for my age from mysterious handbags like the one carried by Mary Poppins. When I was eight years old, *The Lion, the Witch, and the Wardrobe*, the first of C.S. Lewis's annual Narnia Chronicles, came out. After my mother died, I read *At the Back of the North Wind* with its mischievous weather goddess taking a lonely boy in her hair to a world behind the visible. Thus the children's librarians of the Toronto Public Library tested their pernicious theories of literacy on me, their living specimen and captive subject.

For I was the ideal wondertale hero in the making. The lonely, wandering children in the German Grimm and the Norwegian Asbjørnsen collections were like me. All my storybook heroes were like me. I felt like the young King Arthur educated by the Faërye Otherworld. Apart from the rough-and-tumble education in heroism at Crescent School, I knew no other way to be a human than what I found in folk tales. How to be a human being is never obvious.

In the real world, my aunt was Alice Kane. Born in 1908, she grew up on stories told by fourteen aunts and uncles on the Pyper side of her family, who kept alive the mixed oral and literary tradition peculiar to Ireland. Photographs of her as a girl show the bratty self-confidence of a Presbyterian child with long red hair, like Anne of Green Gables. Alice was born at the height of an age of wonder that began in the nineteenth century with the Alice of *Alice's Adventures in Wonderland* (1865) and *Alice Through the Looking Glass* (1871). The bookish middle class of Europe and America believed in wonder with the conviction they gave to formal religion. Alice went to the pantomimes and heard a character in *Peter Pan* say: "All the world is made of faith and trust, and pixie dust" and "To die will be an awfully big adventure." She went on to the end of her life believing equally in Christianity and paganism, as if the Bible was one big wondertale and Saint Paul supplied the rules for reading it.

In this, she was preceded by her countrywoman Ella Young, who

Boys and Girls House in the 1930s
(Toronto Public Library Archives)

was born into Ulster Protestantism but moved south, taught herself Gaelic, and became a full-fledged, gun-concealing Irish revolutionary. Ella tells in her biography *Flowering Dusk* of joining Maud Gonne and W.B. Yeats to commune with the spirit of a mountain. She describes the leaders of the Irish National Land League setting apart special land for cooperative dairies to be run by the poverty-stricken farmers, thereby rolling back landlordism. And Gaelic language instructors teaching Irish dancing to children. And poets directing shop girls to act in pageants about the ancient gods. After the defeat of the moderate nationalists in 1924, Ella left Ireland to teach Irish mythology at Berkeley – to be detained at Ellis Island in New York because the immigration officials thought she was insane. She told them she believed in fairies. And Alice Kane? Born in the age of the *art nouveau* wondertale, she was a perfect choice to work in the home which wonder literature created for itself: libraries designed exclusively for children.

Miss Smith must have known on sight that this rebellious upstart would be happier working far away from head office, with its hierarchy of Seniors, Juniors, and "Infants." Alice was posted to Toronto's West End where her storytelling skills fit with the Slavic and Jewish children who had storytelling in their culture and were told stories at home. "Those children sat looking at you dreamily, and they wept when the story was sad and smiled when it was happy, and they remembered and asked for more, and the longer the story was the more they liked it. They never had enough of stories. I could tell them stories all day."

She came to Canada in 1921, the year of the greatest immigrant wave to date in proportion to Canada's population. That same year brought a Jewish boy who spoke no English. David Lewis would be her classmate at McGill, then a Rhodes Scholar, then organizer and eventually Parliamentary Leader of the social democratic movement in Canada. Alice was noticed at McGill for more than her vivid hair, though Sir Arthur Currie, the Principal of the University who had commanded the Canadian Corps in the Great War, remarked on it at every opportunity. She took courses with the worthies of the time, including Steven Leacock for Political Economy. From McGill, she went to Toronto at the start of the Depression, and was appointed to the Toronto Public Library to do what she did best, which was tell stories.

What did I learn from her stories? I learned how to travel light and not possess things. It was the witches, ogres, trolls and other single-minded obsessives who hoarded; they hoarded wealth and lost children. Usually oral stories don't spell out strict moral choices, and their nature spirits tend to be morally ambiguous. While a fairy tale dragon is a fire-spewing evil for no reason, a wondertale dragon is likely to have a good reason for behaving like an angry volcano: a dragon is the spirit of a mountain, those precious jewels and minerals are rightly theirs. Unlike a fairy tale which is written for children, an oral wondertale is told to adults by a storyteller who isn't concerned with defining *what* is good and *what* is evil so much as *how* to choose the right thing to do when you don't know what's right or wrong in a strange situation.

In times past there lived a king and queen who said to each other, "Would that we had a child!" yet they had not. But it happened once ... Recalling her voice today, I believe it was the rightness in the way Alice told a story that helped me make ethical choices throughout my life. Rightness? I mean that her words held together in just the right way. They felt as if they could be said no other way. They had balance, proportion, harmony.

These are misunderstood terms because over their long battered history they came to be confused with a properly functioning hierachical society, with everyone in their right place as prescribed by the guardians of morality. But in classical cultures (Asian as well as European), finding a harmony or balance isn't about following rules. It's intuiting the right relationship independent of the rules for social conformity and often outside them altogether. A person instinctively arranges flowers in a vase. "There! That feels right!" This example comes from Japan, where it's said it isn't the flowers but the spaces between the flowers that are important. A judge feels that the punishment spelled out in law is out of proportion to the crime committed by the accused, who has otherwise led a blameless life. Taking this extenuating circumstance into account, the judge intuits a milder punishment, one that better fits the circumstances. Aristotle, who provides this example of "the appropriate" (*to prepon*), adds that judges who bend the law in positive ways ought to be sure their emotions have an internal harmony. From Cicero comes the example of the good public speaker who instead of trotting out the same speech every time changes it to suit the mood and expectations of the listeners. I've heard Alice Kane change a story on the spot to accord with her sense of audience. Her words alter, their tone changes, yet the story retains an overall composure that feels right. "You want the story. Just the story. You can kill things by formalizing them. The story will change every time you tell it," she points out. The classical authors are indicating a power within us we don't have a name for: a merging of instinct and intuition that comes into play when the rules are inadequate or missing. This is the ability to estimate the spaces between the flowers, the distance between a crime and a punishment, the gap between a speaker and a listener. Seeking that unscripted rightness is to go beyond the algorithms of statistical probability. What lies beyond the measuring rule are living relations, and living relations are always in a state of change. How can there be a rule for the changing colours of a sunset?

It seems the ability to make the right judgment in a novel situation is an unconscious skill. "And how miraculous it is!" observed the philosopher A.N. Whitehead. "Even in common speech. I do not mean thoughts we have first carefully formulated in our minds and then given words. I mean quite unconscious thoughts which spring instantaneously from the unconscious into words without any intermediary process being operative that we know of; that is the most amazing thing. It has never been explained, no one knows the connection between these unconscious meditations and their sudden translation into speech." I can't explain it either – clearly, it doesn't want to be talked about. But here's a harmless speculation.

Try walking from room to room in your house with your eyes closed. Do you feel you know roughly where you are in relation to obstacles, other bodies, objects distant and proximate? That sense of "a proper" relationship is your proprioceptive sense (from *proprius* = "one's own" + *capere* = "to grasp"). This is the scientific name for a complex coordination of inputs from several kinds of nerve receptors tuned to a body's position and movement. All moving animals, some insects, and certain fish are known to have this neuro-muscular-sensory power. Also flowering plants, and trees with their mysterious ability to straighten themselves by estimating their curvature in relation to gravity. And human beings, who in complete darkness are able to right themselves against the horizon and walk without losing their balance. Here is the soil in which grows the slender plant of moral uprightness. It is what guides the wondertale hero and heroine as they venture out from the security of home into an unmapped space crowded with ambiguity, treachery, and petulant authority. But also surprising strangers who show the way forward. No accident that the wondertale seekers often acquire an animal guide. Animals navigate a world where they're used to finding what they can't see.

This blind reckoning must have governed the outdoor life of our ancestors when they lived close to the minds and feelings of Earth. Intuition guides behaviour most vividly during what used to be called the wonder years, that is, the years from nine to thirteen when the young adult practices making their own decisions in parent-free situations. For me, at that age, the class of mysterious others I had no scripts for were grown-ups, girls and administrators – people who threatened my dreamy open-spiritedness with a limiting proposition. I think the sense of a living relationship is governed by a subliminal Prime Directive: *Don't let anything come between you and your sense of survival.* For one day, that survival sense will save your life. It saved mine when I was eight years old, lost and alone one night in the mountains of British Columbia.

Sandon was one of the boom towns of the 1880s when gold and silver were discovered in the B.C. interior. At its height, it was the biggest settlement in the province after Vancouver, with several mines and smelters going full blast and twenty-six hotel saloons for the miners. When I came here with my mother, it had become a ghost town with just a few inhabitants. The great mills with their rock-crushing hammers and silver-extracting chemical tanks were silent. Only one thing disturbed the serenity. It was an alpine creek tumbling down the mountainside. It surged through the trees near our rented cottage high above the town. On my first evening in the mountains, my mother took me to see it, probably to point out that it was a hazard along with an abandoned silver mill on its bank. It was a summer evening. Neither of us was prepared for how quickly night falls in the mountains. It drops like a curtain. But this was an idyllic path on soft moss, under overhanging branches. There, in sight of the turbulence, my mother looked me in the eye and said, "Whatever you do – don't go off the path."

Now, readers of tales of wonder and enchantment will recognize these words as the *prohibition* or *negative injunction*, a common plot device usually at the beginning of a story. They warn of a boundary that should not be crossed, an adventure that should not be taken. But in wondertales, prohibitions exist in order to be broken. That is what prohibitions are for. I have a homespun theory, based on my chequered career as a parent, that breaking a prohibition is necessary to becoming your own person. The theory is that at any stage of parenting, a parent will underestimate the child's emotional age; simultaneously, the child will overestimate the parent's emotional age. This ongoing communications gap is called "growing up." "Don't do that!" the parent says. Immediately the child goes off and does the forbidden thing. He has to find out the meaning of the experience for himself; she has to discover her own freedom, because freedom can't be given – it must be taken. So children, enclosed in an infantile paradise, reach for the forbidden fruit and discover the heady freedom of choosing between right and wrong all by themselves. That was why I left the path.

There is a Russian wondertale called "The Boy Who Learned the Meaning of Fear." I learned the meaning of fear that night in the Kootenay mountains.

I learned something else too. This came to me late into the night after I had skirted mine shafts and mountain crevasses, lost under the stars. It occurred to me that I was having an adventure. So I did the proper thing in that situation – I became a hero. First, I found a ready-made club, the root and bole of a small cedar. It wasn't the club made out of an oak tree which Heracles used to knock eight of the nine heads off the giant water snake living in the swamp of Lerna – but it would do. It put the adventure into proportion. Unknown adversaries suddenly shrunk down to figures I could contend with. I didn't anticipate meeting a troll because trolls lived in Norway o'er the foam, and in spite of the silver in the mountains all around I didn't think I'd see a ridge-backed dragon. But I might run into a bear. So I was armed and ready for an adventure. Next I made a lean-to out of planks scattered around the mouth of a mine shaft, a shelter identical to the one in the book *Wildwood Wisdom*. Then, because my situation had a shape, I slept.

Morning peered over a mountain. Where was I? Wherever it was, my sore feet told me that I'd walked forever back and forth along switch-backs and I didn't dare go back into that zigzagging labyrinth. Who was I? I was a hero. But while this status vaguely served my imagination, it didn't tell me what to do. Instead, it invited a complex sense of direction to have its say. I climbed a tree. Where was the town of Sandon? But all I saw, way down in a valley at the bottom of the mountain, was a dirt road. Well, if there's a road, it goes somewhere. I crashed through forest down the mountainside until I reached it. But should I turn left or right? "Turn right," the feeling said. So I turned right instead of left and walked into Sandon in time to join the outer fringe of a search party that was being instructed by a Mountie. Excited tracker dogs began sniffing me and wagging their tails furiously. To my disappointment, the Mountie wasn't wearing the scarlet tunic of the Royal Canadian Mounted Police – he wore a chocolate-coloured tunic, but his breeches were blue and they had the familiar gold stripe.

"Johnny comes marching home again after night in wilderness!"

trumpeted the *New Denver Miner*, echoing a popular radio song. When asked what he was carrying, the boy said it was a club, "in case I meet an adversary."

I survived. The wondertale I was living put me in a place where dreams exceeded fears.

Many years later, I returned to Sandon. The town has picked up since my boyhood visit. There's even a museum and a visitor's information centre. The seven-story high mill has fallen down, but the creek charges down the mountainside, seething with glacial meltwater as before. I remembered the tangy scent of naked ore and saw pebbles sparkling with zinc and silver that had fallen off the transport trucks. You could put one in your pocket as a talisman because the signs told you not to. And yes, here was the mossy path still overhung by cedar boughs, and it led to the cottage on the mountainside, and unbelievably an ancient refrigerator was in use on the porch. Here was where the Mountie carried me on his shoulders to my distraught mother.

I tiptoed back along the mossy forest tunnel to find the place where I'd mischievously slipped into the trees so I could leap out and surprise my mother further along the path. Going off the path and up the slope into the forest, I came across a dirt road once used by the trucks carrying ore to the mill. I had turned left and run along this road, intending to cut back into the trees and jump out in front of her. But now I saw the mistake I'd made just as the evening dropped behind a mountain. The road led straight to the abandoned mill beside the cascade roaring down through the forest. *I feel mist on my face. I have to get far away from this!* I ran to put the danger behind me, not realizing that I had taken a switchback. Frightened, I ran back and forth along a series of switchbacks that led me more and more up the mountain and more and more to the west. I came to an entrance to a silver mine with rusting ore buckets, and this sign of human activity in the wilderness brought me to a halt. That was where I came to my senses.

The event, as I retraced it in my mind that day, released itself to join the layers of stillness that make up a present-day ghost town. That is where I left it. What I carried away was a question I have fondled for a lifetime. How is it that a person can often make the right choice spontaneously, without relying on rules or precedents?

I've said the answer is some inborn ability to estimate the quality of a relationship. It is educated in a person by folk tales, vision quests, wondertales, hero stories, myths — the ancient storytelling forms that preserve a memory of moving about in nature. It is the birthright of our existence in the measures of Earth. People say that aesthetic judgment is useless. Don't believe it! Beauty saves lives. It saved mine one night long ago in the Kootenay mountains.

The worldspin

It's supposed the first people up and about are the emergency shift workers – the nurses, doctors, ambulance drivers, fire fighters, police – the ones who keep us safe. But the true harbingers of each new day are the elderly. Long before the public service workers are awake, the elderly are watching the world come alive in *The Guardian* and on CNN.

Soon cars will jam the highways feeding into the cities. Over four thousand domestic and international flights will crisscross the skies of America. Some four hundred container ships and ferries will traverse the English Channel, regulated by a helicopter on traffic patrol. The spectacle of a world in motion will continue until nightfall, when things quieten down – but its guardians are still alert. At 7:30 in Britain, a technician will watch for a spike in demand for electricity as close to three million kettles come to a boil after a popular TV show. The technician will shunt megawatts from France to get Britain through the next four to six minutes without the power grid collapsing.

What are we doing so early in the day, the wide-awake elderly? We are attending to our mortality. Any prescriptions up for renewal? These are what keep us even-tempered and docile. Otherwise we'd rise up in a fury against the injustices of the world and unite in a geriatric revolution. We are the fastest-growing age group in Canada. There are 7.6 million of us. In twenty years, we will be eleven million – that's one in four people. We want doctors! We want nurses! Don't mess with us.

Any medical appointments today? Check the yellow Post-it on the bathroom mirror just under the six emergency phone numbers.

Now let's see who died overnight ... no one we know, only a couple of secondary rock stars and an actor. Then we check the people we care about.

Mine are, first, Barbara von Otter in Sweden, my oldest friend. I've known her since we were teenagers in Toronto a million years ago. She has a slow-growing but inoperable tumour at the back of her brain which causes her to see double. The visual disturbance can be corrected by finding the right lens, but nothing can be done about the tumour. She has talked about flying over for Owen and Natasha's wedding in the fall. I don't know if she'll be able to make it.

Next there is the irrepressible storyteller and wit Professor William Blissett who is approaching his 103rd birthday. His existence is ridiculous, beautiful, and unfair. He has kept in good health by being single, making his work his hobby, and trusting in the One Holy Apostolic Church to take care of any troublesome thoughts. Right now, he's reading the *Globe and Mail* after hearing it go thud against his apartment door. He hasn't watched television since his TV set blew up in 1964. He has lived in his apartment overlooking the Don Valley since then, to the frustration of every new owner of his building intent on raising the rents. They can't raise his. He enjoys the protection of the lease he signed back in the twentieth century.

Then there's my son Owen whom you've already met, and his partner, Natasha. She's just driven off to work in the Critical Care Unit of a hospital somewhere – one of the thousands of emergency workers who keep our lives secure.

The world is a spin and I'm in it. I can't go off seeking adventure in travel the way I used to. But I can dream.

4
THE DREAM OF THE OPEN ROAD

Railway trains charged through my childhood. Living one block away from the CPR tracks that crossed the top of the Toronto Annex, I was aware night and day of these important trains that carried freight across a big land. They were pulled by obedient monsters panting and puffing in the distance, then clanging their drive shafts rhythmically as they went by, leaving a pall of coal smoke. Where did they go, those busy trains?

Later, as a teenager on Summerhill Gardens, I lived a block north of this railway. It crossed the nearby ravine, taking me to my girlfriend Agneta waiting at the other end of the bridge. Then it went on to span the Don Valley, eventually following the top of the Escarpment to the city of Peterborough where I now live, a block away from those same CPR tracks. The romantic steam engine was replaced with the boring diesel by Neil Crump, the great president of the Canadian Pacific Railway, who began as a lineman and couldn't travel on one of his trains without scanning the wheels of a train going in the opposite direction for a hot axle box. My first wonder was transportation.

Wonder was fulfilled when my parents began sending me alone on the overnight train to Montreal to stay with my grandparents over Christmas. I boarded clutching a handwritten note by Crump which I showed to amused sleeping car porters who transformed seats magically into bunks. The letter identified me as the only child in Canada permitted to travel unescorted on the CPR. My grandfather had taken me into Mr. Crump's office and proudly introduced me. As former Director of Shipping for Canada's eastern ports, he distributed the freight that Crump sent him.

The excitement! I'd snuggle into the starched linen sheets under the heavy brown blanket and peek out at snow-covered fields and sudden highway crossings with stop lights flashing and bells ringing, until lulled to sleep by the clickety-clack of the wheels over the rail joins.

The CPR ruled! With its stately maroon and gold livery, it was superior to the olive and gold CNR. I knew it was superior from my grandfather's expostulations over the *Montreal Gazette* at breakfast to the effect that the Canadian National Railway was owned by a short-sighted entity called "the government" which had a tendency to appoint its friends to high places in transportation.

My grandfather had been a sailor during the last years of the great sailing ships. Together, we used to wind up the weights on the grandfather clock to an anchor-weighing song sung by sailors circling the capstan. It consisted of verses made up by each in turn, with all joining in the chorus. My grandfather bellowed:

> *Once I loved an Irish girl*
> *but she was fat and lazy.*

And I joined in:

> *Away, haul away —*
> *Haul away together.*
> *Away, haul away.*
> *Haul away Joe!*

That was every Sunday. Promptly at 1:00 p.m., the three clocks in the house chimed to the beginning of the long dash of the Dominion Time Signal broadcast by CBC Radio.

The young Hugh Smiley Kane transitioned from sail to steam to

"McAndrew's Hymn," a meditation by a Scottish Chief Engineer in a poem by Rudyard Kipling:

> *Lord, Thou hast made this world below the shadow of a dream,*
> *An' taught by time, I tak' it so — exceptin' always Steam.*
> *From coupler-flange to spindle-guide I see Thy Hand, O God —*
> *Predestination in the stride of o' yon connectin'-rod.*

My aunt Alice explained to me that Kipling's mother was Scottish — that was why he wrote storybooks about fairies alongside jingoistic verse about the British Empire. She quoted a verse by a now forgotten parodist:

> *Down in some Tooting iron and brick yard*
> *Lives the poet known as Rudyard.*
> *Meanwhile through the forest stripling*
> *Moves the faun the gods call Kipling.*

Hugh Kane's first command

Kipling saw that one of the Empire's greatest gifts to civilization was that it provided employment to thousands of young men from the Celtic fringe of the British Isles: Ireland, Scotland, Cornwall, and Wales. These same young men, rising into positions of command in the Merchant Navy, developed an ethical shorthand based on Kipling. "*Wangarti at the worst – an' damn all patent fuel!*" referred to the coal loaded at the top of New Zealand for the run across the Pacific. It meant what's good enough is good enough, and probably cheaper. Every Christmas, former ship captains who had retired in Montreal gathered around my grandfather's dinner table to smoke their pipes, play cribbage, and recite Rudyard Kipling. Yards and yards of Kipling.

My grandfather left the town of Larne in Northern Ireland at the age of sixteen to go to sea. He rose to command a deep sea freighter of the Ulster Steamship Company at the age of thirty-six. During the early years of Marconi radio, he signed his Morse Code messages with the word *Slainthe*. It's a toast in Irish, but ship captains across the North Atlantic took it to mean "Captain Slainthe." They recalled that during the 1914–1918 war, when all shipping was restricted out of the port of Dover, Slainthe slipped harbour and zig-zagged through the ring of German U-boats rather than pay the additional docking fee. In 1924, when the dream of a United Ireland free of both Westminster and the Vatican was no longer possible, he came ashore and became Director of Shipping for Canada's eastern ports. He put his daughter Alice into Netherwood School for girls and his son Hugh into Rothesay School for boys, both close to Saint John, New Brunswick, the winter port. (By a triumph of the Protestant imagination, Hugh and Alice Kane named their children after themselves.) He bought a house in Montreal and turned its basement into a Marine Museum where I spent hours reading books about life at sea, surrounded by ships in glass cases, a portrait of Lord Nelson, circular tables intricately carved in India, and the bric-à-brac of Empire.

Alice Kane early in her marriage

At Westmount Station on a winter morning, several steam locomotives are sending spumes of smoke straight up into the crisp air. My grandfather is waiting on the platform. He's wearing a three-piece suit with a watch chain across his vest. No overcoat. He doesn't talk. Instead, he takes me up to admire the locomotive. And, as soon as we're back home, he shows a wooden model he made for me of a Pacific and Orient ocean liner, painted black with the distinctive P & O white horizontal line along the top of the hull, and named *Khiva* in fine white lettering. He doesn't know how to talk to a child but he knows how my imagination works. It works just like his. He has the imagination of a child.

It was inevitable that when I turned sixteen he'd send me to sea.

I had long prepared myself for this. I'd read the bible titled *Manual of Seamanship* with its wisdom set in catechisms: Question: "What to do if found upon a lee shore?" Answer: "The good Master will not allow himself to be found in this condition." I had memorized the Top Secret 1914–1918 Admiralty zig-zag charts in a book with a leaded-weighted cover so it could be thrown over the side if the ship was boarded. I knew from *The Ship Captain's Medical Guide* how to perform an appendectomy at sea, and how to treat syphilis ("Bathe the affected parts in Potassium Permanganate Solution"). In short, I was ready to serve in an up-to-date modern ship. As well, I'd been taken in tow by my grandfather to explore freighters loading in Montreal, while he reminisced with their captains and drank whiskey which was forbidden at home. He enjoyed especially the Ellerman-Wilson ships because of the curry served at lunch. Checking out the stern of the *City of Benares*, I met a Lascar – lascar, ac-

Late in his career
as an Ulster Steamship captain

cording to the discrimination at the time, was the name for a sailor from India – naked except for a loincloth and a turban, grinding curry powder in a mortar and pestle. We grinned at each other, so far apart as to be wonders. I was entrusted to an officer cadet who explained a sextant ("Don't ever drop the captain's sextant") and took me around the Engine Room. It was quiet here with the steam turbines at rest, away from the rattle of the steam pistons driving the winches of the ship's cranes as they hoisted freight into the hold. Once on another ship when no one was looking I climbed the foremast to the Crow's Nest. So I already knew my way around the *Carrigan Head*, the newest of the Ulster Steamship Line freighters, all named after prominent headlands around the coast of Ireland. William Haddock, its captain, had once been an officer under Captain Kane, but my grandfather's parting words were in the presence of Mr. Crawford, the First Mate: "Do whatever this man tells you, and don't listen to anyone else."

The apprentice officers, technically Uncertified Junior Officers, had two cabins on the port side aft, at the end of the officers' corri-

Carrigan Head, port side freshly painted, loading paper in Port-Alfred (now the city of Saguenay) at the head of the Saguenay River.
(Sean Kane photo)

dor. Over on the starboard side were the engineering officers. They kept to themselves. Once at sea, everybody was absorbed into the routine of ship's watches. The common language – silence; the main sound – the forced air system; the main sensation – the thudding of the propellers; the smells – salt sea air, oil, paint, boiled potatoes.

Night at sea: I am on the Captain's watch managed in his absence by the Third Officer. An easy swell. All the stars are out. The wheel house is dark, except for the pink light of the compass reflected on the face of the helmsman. No one has said a word for the past hour. But it's coming up to 22:00. Time to make hot cocoa for the watch. Don't forget the lookout on the port wing of the bridge. The Third Officer checks the ship's clock and disappears into the Chart Room to initial the next course correction on our Great Circle route (there's no direct straight line to a destination on a map because of the curved surface of the Earth). He returns and whispers something to Peter Dobbs, the senior cadet, who summons me with his finger. Down a steep ladder staircase to the Engine Room, so warm after the bridge deck. We go around reminding everybody to re-set their watches one hour. Then behind the two turbines to the propeller shaft where another ladder with handrails ascends to an outside door at the back of the boat. Here the "log," a rotating propeller on a line thrown over the stern, measures off the distance travelled. This rough reckoning will be revised by the captain with his sextant at high noon, if there's a sun.

Against this backdrop of silent, ritual duty, human oddity stands out.

In the Officer's Wardroom there's an old chair that belongs to "Chips," the Ship's Carpenter. His main duty as far as I can tell is to measure the ship's water supply by dropping a plumb line through a hole in the deck. This he's done daily since time began, taking his favourite chair with him from ship to ship. Chips is an object lesson for not spending your life at sea. The Third Mate has already confided that he intends to quit and become a police constable in

Birkenhead. He points to a furrow in the wooden arm rest of Chip's chair. "Jayzuschrist, can you believe that? – that was made by his arm sliding back and forth to the motion of the ship." His remark sounds like a wail of desperation.

At Trois Rivières, it's discovered I can speak French. Suddenly, I have an important duty. Tell the dockworkers loading rolled paper into the hold not to smoke. A sixteen-year-old gives his first command at sea: "*S'il voux plait, monsieur – ne fumez pas ici. Nous conveyons le blé. Le ... er, DUST. C'est explosif.*" To my astonishment, the stevedore promptly crushes his cigarette with his work boot.

At Quebec City, we come upon a group of warships from several countries. They're here to celebrate the opening of the St. Lawrence Seaway which will allow ocean-going freighters to dock in Chicago. There's shore leave for the crew. I stand gangway duty, the role of an officer apprentice. Late at night, the seamen return with an American sailor's hat. It's a trophy from a brawl. Next day comes the message: they want it back.

Departing Quebec City in the morning, we see a U.S. submarine moored on the far shore. I notice the Stars and Stripes on a staff at its stern. "Isn't the Merchant Marine supposed to salute a warship?" I ask innocently.

"Why not?" the First Mate says. It's a short walk to the stern to lower the Red Ensign. Over on the sub, a sailor appears hurriedly on the conning tower, scrambles down the footholds on its side, races to the stern, detaches the flag staff from its socket, holds the flag briefly across his chest, then reattaches the portable flagstaff. He returns to the conning tower, shaking his head in consternation. He isn't wearing a hat. This brings jeers from our crew. One of them is wearing his hat.

★ ★ ★

At Lac Saint Jean at the top of the Saguenay River, the cadets are given the day off. We take the ship's rowboat and go ashore, to look down from a hilltop at the crew painting the port side of the boat and touching up the white Ulster Steamship Line lettering. Why only the left side? My grandfather's voice:

> *Red to red, go straight ahead.*
> *But green to green should never be seen.*

We're passing someone important tomorrow.

Moving ever so slowly beneath the ancient cliffs of the Saguenay River, we watch the Royal Yacht *Britannia* approach behind two of the new Canadian destroyer escorts. I identify them to the surprise of the First Officer: the *Kootenay* and the *Gatineau*. A tiny figure wearing a red dress emerges on the afterdeck of the *Britannia*. The Queen. She waves, then stays outside to admire us until the British stern escort comes into view. It is HMS *Ulster*. I hope they admire our paint job too.

At Rimouski, a motorboat crashes through a steep swell to take the Pilot ashore. We rig the side ladder. But first a girl wearing jeans and a fisherman's wool sweater climbs up. Hotshit! A girl! Dark hair in a bob, crazy eyes. She could be Québécoise or Irish. Or both. Captain Haddock steers her out of view. She must be the daughter of someone important in the company (the Ulster Steamship Line is 50 percent owned by McLean-Kennedy Shipping Agents in Montreal, though the boats are built and staffed in Belfast).

This voyage now has a distraction.

★ ★ ★

Nosing through fog on the Gulf of St. Lawrence, we double the watch and sound our horn regularly. The First Mate takes lookout on the bow. Not far from here, the *Empress of Ireland* hit a Norwegian freighter and went down in fourteen minutes, taking around a thousand passengers with her. I join Mr. Crawford. He doesn't take his binoculars off the fog. A shape could loom instantly. I squint into the invisible. Wicked shapes. I start seeing shapes. Shapes everywhere.

Captain Haddock brings the girl to have lunch with the officer cadets: Peter Dobbs, John Ritchie, Ted Hayes, and myself. We have a small wardroom which we bring our food trays to from the galley. The girl stares at an enormous serving of Irish sausages, French fries, and Brussels sprouts. She knows a better world than this, but she digs in gamely and makes pleasant conversation without revealing a single thing about herself except her age. She's nineteen. Out of my league, but not beyond Peter Dobbs who is casual and blonde and has already bedded a Québécoise girl I offered a cigarette to in French. But not a flicker of interest in our guest's eyes. She's been placed far away from us in the special guest room, port side just aft of the bridge.

Apprentice officers work side-by-side with the crew on Head Line steamers, which means we come under the command of the Bosun, who sets menial tasks. Clean the seepage out of a compartment under the paint store, above the propeller. John Ritchie and I clung with our mops to a ladder going straight down through a dark hole. The tiny, low-ceilinged, fetid place rose over twenty feet with the pitching of the ship, making my knees buckle; then it plummeted like a broken elevator, making me float in the air. Whereupon I contributed my vomit to the sewage, not sparing Ritchie.

★ ★ ★

Outdoor work. We've reached the Gulf Stream bringing warm water and a temperate climate to northern Europe. Dolphins surf our bow wave. Everybody's mood soars, and in the general good will I'm forgiven for puking all over John Ritchie. But I'm not yet a fellow seaman. The Bosun addresses me for the first time. "Lash that up, sailor." His eyes twinkle. He is being laconic. I analyse a pile of splintered timber that was once fenders for protecting the ship's side while docking.

The Bosun's name is Alaru. He's said to be a Count from one of the Baltic States, and he has the dignity of an aristocrat. But his inwardness is that of an intellectual. Who knows what he's thinking in his silences? A story is that he was hosing down the deck one day when a group of well-dressed women with young children came up the gangplank for the Captain's reception...

"Ach! Vomen and children!" Alaru said turning the hose on them full blast.

I find rope in Paint Storage and return to the wood pile. Alaru is still staring at it as if it's an offence to shipboard order, like women and children, and possibly myself. I bundle it up and finish with a good, tight knot.

The Bosun stares at it curiously. He waves an older seaman over.

"By God, that's a Carrick Bend. I haven't seen one of them for forty years."

The Bosun gives me a nod. A rare compliment. The knot was common in the old days for reefing sails. I used to practice tying my grandfather's shoelaces with Carrick Bends.

On duty as lookout on the wing of the bridge, I sense I am being watched. The girl without a name. She's been inspecting me. She looks away quickly. We watch the Atlantic swells together, not speaking.

★ ★ ★

"That's Donegal!"

We were painting the superstructure. Home was in sight. Wives and sweethearts. But not everybody's home. Count Alaru didn't have a home. Ted Hayes lived in Dublin and, meeting up with him another summer on the *Bengore Head*, he took me by foot down Grafton Street, across Stephen's Green, then down to Blackrock where his huge family lived. That night I was embraced by a large beachside party with people of all ages stripping down and swimming in the sea. Catholics have all the fun.

The Coxswain looked up at me on the ladder painting. "We need the key to the Storm Locker."

I looked at the Bosun to confirm. Count Alaru looked away. Beneath his dignity.

"Try the Engine Room. It's at the end of a long weight."

No one in the Engine Room knew who had the key last. They looked at each other earnestly and shook their heads.

"You might try the Galley. I think Cook uses the Storm Locker to store his potatoes."

The Cook had a reputation for sketchy initiatives. Once when the crew went ashore to a working men's restaurant in Baltimore, they told the chef that their ship's cook stole from the food budget. He did this by under-ordering key staples, such as eggs. He could make an omelet for the entire crew using just three eggs. The restaurant cook immediately took off his apron and started down to the ship to get the recipe.

No sign of the Cook, but the Galley had an assistant who was pale and pimply from staying indoors. Mostly he peeled potatoes using an electric peeler fastened to the wall. That was what he was doing when I asked where the missing key was.

"I don't know where the fuckin' thing is. It 'taint here, mate."

Back on deck, Mr. Crawford was inspecting my paintwork.

"Excuse me, sir. I went to look for the key to the Storm Locker."

The First Mate smiled. "Forget about it, son."

I grimaced. I'd forgotten my grandfather's prime directive. Don't do anything anyone tells you, except the First Officer. Second lesson: the Irish can't be happy without thinking up some mischief.

"Kane to the bridge."

We were rounding the top of County Antrim in a rain squall. The sea was choppy. Captain Haddock had summoned me.

He was taking the ship in close. I heard crashing surf as each headland went by. Their brooding shapes through the mix of rain and fog. So bleak and forbidding. I wiped the spray off my face.

"The land of your ancestors," the captain said.

Liverpool. Nudged up Merseyside against an ebb tide by ancient pre-War tugboats blowing coal smoke in our faces. The tidal bore is significant here.

"It goes up and down like a whore's drawers," the Third Officer observes sourly. He looks away from Birkenhead. "That's the Liver Building. See those birds on top?"

I pick out the huge golden statues.

"If they see a virgin, they flap their wings."

According to the gossip, this port is hot. Later in the day, I'll pass girls walking in pairs wearing signature tight floor-length skirts. They call me "luv" and "darling." They're my age.

But I feel at home here for my own special reason. I can identify the ships in port from my grandfather's two-volume *Shipping Wonders of the World*. There's a real P & O cargo liner, half freighter, half passenger ship, with two decks of elegant balconies allowing fresh air on the run through the Suez Canal, then across to India. That's where we get the word *posh* for preferred travellers. It was written in chalk on their luggage. "Port Out, Starboard Home." And there's a Blue Funnel liner, the *Telemachus*. The Blue Funnel line ships were named after Greek heroes and looked manly with their straight vertical masts and funnels.

After we dock – a tricky business because we edge first into a "basin" or containment area for ships – I go up to the monkey island atop the wheelhouse for a better view. I use the binoculars to find a route up to the esplanade where there's said to be skiffle groups – early rock played to the beat of thimbles on a washboard and a single metal wire attached to an upside-down bucket and controlled by the variation of a stick. The route looks safe. The Merseyside is said to be relaxed compared to Glasgow where there are roving gangs with razor blades on the brims of their hats which they throw like a discus, and fish hooks underneath their lapels so you can't grab them.

Someone's coming up the ladder.

She reaches the top and steps up on the riser holding the outside steering wheel.

I don't remember much of our conversation. I passed her the wheelhouse binoculars and identified neighbouring ships. We must have talked about the last war, because she surveyed the bomb damage, still unrepaired. No, she couldn't come and listen to the skiffle groups. See? – she was dressed for travel. She was getting a train to London.

She just wanted to come up and say goodbye.

She put her arm casually around the brass binnacle. I'd polished it just this morning.

"Well, I guess it's goodbye then," I said.

"Yes, I'm really sorry about that."

"?"

"Hug!"

"Okay."

She stepped around the binnacle and we hugged. And we hugged some more. And...

And then we kissed. And all the kisses we never had and never will have were poured into that one timeless kiss. Timeless, because it was intended for memory. I thought all the ships in the harbour were going to blow their whistles in salute.

"I'm not nineteen," she said. "I'm sixteen – same as you."

My life is punctuated by mysterious women – gatekeepers to the next freedom.

That summer I worked on a Head Line freighter was like no other. I followed the allure of the open road, the "sail road" (*segl rad*) as it's called in Anglo Saxon heroic verse. Later, in the Sixties, young people would take the open road to the West Coast, but my passage into maturity was always over water. Two years later, I signed on to the *Bengore Head* – the name of my grandfather's first command, but not the same ship. And my grandfather, feeling that same tugging at his heart, took a voyage up the newly open Great Lakes to Chicago on board the *Fair Head*. He said he wanted "one last fling." The photographs of the trip show that he had the time of his life.

The old sea dog learned some tricks. He learned how to navigate by radar, how to talk on ship-to-shore radio, how to stay up late with the deck crew watching TV between locks. Captain Kane couldn't sleep anyway because they failed to ring off the hours of the watch on the ship's bell: *ding-ding, ding-ding, ding-ding* (the custom was restored). He stole the metal tab of the key to the Drying Room. Oh, if only they had a warmed room for your wet clothes on a sailing ship!

He must have known that summer of 1960 that he was dying, but he didn't tell us. He died on the fourteenth of May, 1961. The open road.

How couples met

Owen and Natasha's wedding date is set. It's August 11. Invitations are going out to 130 guests, all close to the bridal couple – no notables invited for décor. This is going to be a generational get-together ending in a nightclub dance. The place is to be the venerable Broadview Hotel, a hunk of Victoriana in downtown Toronto.

They met on the Queen's University dating site. Owen registered himself as soon as he passed his Ph.D. Comps; Natasha, then in Medical School, checked the site for the last time. It seems normal that news of their pending marriage followed by wedding invites should go out on a website, with portraits of the well-dressed couple gazing fondly at each other in a wilderness setting. Then five bridesmaid's photos, each with a self-introduction. And the same with the five groomsmen. No pictures of parents. This was considered, but dropped, probably after analysing the photo submitted by the father of the groom who has never successfully made eye-contact with another human being, let alone a camera. So there's a suspicion of passive resistance lurking in the groom's parents. The troubling fact is they never bothered to get married. Like many in their generation, they regarded formal marriage as a trap involving two fixed genders and one main goal, producing children. Many had witnessed their parents twisting and turning inside a double straitjacket before finally getting divorced.

This wasn't Kel's case or mine: our respective parents soldiered on, held together by inertia, familiarity, and their free-spirited children. It was when Kelly suggested that she'd bring a broom to the wedding, throw it on the aisle, grab my hand, and jump, that the future bride and groom began to fear mischief.

This kind of gesture is typical of the spontaneities of the *free to be you, free to be me* generation. Our history together began with Kel's suggestion that I fly out to the West Coast and meet her at the ferry dock in Nanaimo, where she'd be waiting with a truck and camper. It belonged to her parents who were given to driving across Canada on a whim, dropping in on a game of euchre being played non-stop since the Fifties near Lafleche in Saskatchewan. I scarcely knew Kelly when she made the suggestion. After three weeks exploring Vancouver Island, listening to radio station CFUN ("sea-fun"), two people are likely to be pretty sure of whether or not they ought to share a future together. If there was any doubt, confirmation came that night on the beach at Hornby Island ("Welcome to Paradise," the deckhand on the ferry said as we disembarked). We listened to the surf crashing and watched the beam of the Three Sisters lighthouse – a constant in Kel's childhood. Then, suddenly, the first shooting star – too quick to make a wish. But there were more, many more; they came every half minute, and we heard the sizzle they make as they burn out in the atmosphere. I said a silent, inner "I do." That was the Pleiades meteorite shower of August 11.

> *When the stars threw down their spears*
> *And water'd heaven with their tears.*

The same night of the year as Owen and Natasha's wedding.

5
THE DREAM OF FIRST LOVE

Many a time I think to seek
One or the other out and speak
Of that old Georgian mansion, mix
Pictures of the mind, recall
That table and the talk of youth,
Two girls in silk kimonos, both
Beautiful, one a gazelle.
— W.B. Yeats

Innocent affection joined with sexual wonder may not be possible in our savvy online age. I discovered it with Agneta, and our time together stayed lodged in us well into adulthood. It became a touchstone for judging the worth of later intimate relationships and toying with returning to a couple.

But that was in the late 1950s. The first wave of the Baby Boom had hit the age of sixteen. Radios broadcast a sentimentalized puppy love, with themes of "going steady" and "heartbreak." Immature longing was in the air, charged by hormonal urges, sanctioned by conformity, and exploited by TV and popular music. Those of us who couldn't relate to the anodyne sentiment had to wait for Bob Dylan to come to the rescue. But occasionally a song struck a chord of true innocence, like Sonny James' 1956 single about "Young love, first love," with its "true devotion" and "deep emotion."

So that's the secret to our parents' intimacy, we thought. That is why they emit strange animal sounds toward nightfall.

Up to this point, girls for me were an alien race of articulate, physically coordinated extroverts. It was girls who took the initiative, kissing with exaggerated passion in a dark cupboard of the basement rec room, leaving the taste of strawberry-flavoured lipstick. It was girls who controlled the pace of a relationship, which they did by staged tactical retreats until a hand was permitted to cross the world's longest undefended border.

This, despite what I'd recently witnessed as a sailor, was my state of sexual maturity when I wandered into Murphy's Drug Store at Woodlawn and Yonge and saw two Branksome Hall girls in kilts at the pop cooler.

One was Cathy, my neighbour. The other was a silent, self-possessed individual with high cheekbones, a flattened nose, and pierced ears – first time I saw that! Teenage strangers don't give much away. Instead, they communicate telepathically:

Oh, here's an interesting looking boy, and he's from a private school!
Here's an exotic girl. I'd like to know her better!

It seemed, Cathy explained later, that her new friend Barbara had recently arrived from Sweden. And there wasn't just her – there were more of them. Four sisters: named alphabetically: Agneta, Barbara, Caroline, and Diana. Their parents were obviously mirthful.

Soon after, Cathy was invited to bring me to their house. A teenage get-together on a rainy afternoon – one of those occasions when parents simply throw the kids into a room and let them sort themselves out. So long as there's talking and music playing, everything's okay; if silence, then it's time to produce the plate of cookies. But in this case, it was hard to get conversation going. It squeezed out that I'd spent the summer working on a boat between Montreal and Liverpool. But I didn't look like a seaman. For proof I displayed the scar on my finger left by the loose wire on a backspring, the wound metal cable rolled onto winches for pulling a boat into a dock before throwing the mooring ropes.

Silent curiosity. The music played on...

Suddenly, the door opened and the Swedish nanny appeared,

shyly holding Diana in her arms. But this wasn't the *au pair*, whose name was Ulla – this was the older sister. And she was my age.

There followed attempts to pronounce her name correctly: *Aeng – nyet –ta*. And explain the family name, *von Otter*. I got the impression that the family had a long lineage, because the main room of what she called her "farm house" back in Sweden had gold otters painted on the ceiling. Offering these facts, Agneta wasn't confident in speaking. Her English would develop over the winter, but at the beginning she had to rely on her memory of an out-of-date Swedish primary-school textbook:

"Why do you say, *It's raining cats and dogs*? That is silly. Cats and dogs dropping from the clouds."

"We don't say that anymore."

"Oh, I see."

Autumn passed, and the event of meeting this lean, shy girl passed with it. I saw little of Barbara during that time. One evening, a carefully rehearsed voice was on the phone. This is Aeng – nyet – ta. Would I wish to consider to be her date for the Branksome Hall Snowflake Formal? Not being much of a dancer, I mumbled my way out of it. But a cable had been cast.

We started meeting after school at Fran's Restaurant at Yonge and St. Clair, where the private school students ate waffles with cinnamon and maple syrup and drank chocolate milkshakes so thick that the straw stuck straight up. We walked the bending streets of Rosedale, ties loosened, our bodies bumping together. I taught her English; she taught me Swedish. I learned to say *bra* ("good") and *bysthållare* ("bra"). Unsure in conversation, we defaulted to the first language of humanity. The first language is touch. Surely Adam and Eve spoke touch at their shy, awkward meeting in Paradise.

I soon learned that for Agneta an important experience needed to be assimilated to custom. This often had the effect of ritual. Meeting my father, she made a curtsy. When she described to me the words of a folk song we heard on a Swedish film – it was played on a radio in the wheelhouse of a ship at night – she crossed her legs, straightened her back, and began to narrate like a storyteller. The song was a popular folktale in Sweden at the time.

"Once there was a princess," she said. "She lived in a valley at the bottom of a mountain. And so tall was that mountain that its top was always covered in cloud. Suitors came to court the princess. She said to them this: 'At the top of that mountain there is a flower. It is a white flower. No one has ever seen it. Go and climb the mountain and bring to me that white flower.'

"The suitors looked at her. They looked at the mountain. Its sides were steep, steep, steep. So they said, 'No way am I going to climb that mountain for you.'

"But one day came a young man – he was a handsome young man. She told him what she had told the others: 'Climb to the top, and bring to me the white flower which grows there.'

" 'Yes. I'll do that,' he said. "Of course, I will.'

"He goes to climb the mountain, and she goes back to her work which is spinning wool. She is not concerned at him. Some of the suitors who tried to climb the mountain for her quit and came back empty-handed.

"But he climbed. He climbed and he climbed.

And she became concerned. You see, she rather liked this one. He seemed so confident. He'd been climbing for so long. She looked up at the top of the mountain covered in cloud. She couldn't see him.

"But then she heard a cry. Had he slipped and fallen? She went running to the bottom of the mountain. And there he was on the ground. He was dead. His blood was all around.

"And there, in his hand was the flower that no one has ever seen. But the flower in his hand wasn't white. It was red. It was stained with his blood."

Agneta smiled wistfully.

Love-making was also framed as a ritual. It began when she

let down her hair. She unfastened the clip holding it in a roll, and shook her hair free so it fell over her shoulders. This was her way of giving consent.

Going out on a date, I never knew was what going to happen. The Ingmar Bergman film *Wild Strawberries* played out its *angst* in monochromatic slow motion to a silent, absorbed audience of intellectuals, sensitive to every nuance. The scene changed.

"*That's my farm!*" Agneta cried. "*Look! There's my farm.*"

People in the audience applauded. It seemed the scene was shot at Stora Hultrum with its lake.

Agneta at Stora Hultrum

Teenage love is unconditional acceptance, matter-of-fact loyalty, and an urgent need to be together. Agneta was a playful friend who couldn't frown when she tried and smelled of cardamom. Summer separated us: she took a position as family helper at a cottage on an island in Georgian Bay. Our relationship poured into handwritten letters.

It's hard to imagine today in a world chronically short of time why two young people would write long handwritten letters to each other that said absolutely zero. But love letters come from the soul, and the soul makes its own time. And space, for the private letter was a refuge where a couple could share problems and feelings they were too tongue-tied to express. If there was nothing to say, that was alright: the point of the letter wasn't to convey news; it was to renew a bond. So a letter usually began by describing the setting where it was being written – a rock overlooking the bay – this brought the reader and the writer together. Then came the drivel:

> You are quite right when you think that "Kära" means "Dear". I just can't see how you can pick up so much Swedish. Now that you know what Dear is in Swedish you might as well learn what Dearest is. It is "Käraste".
> And please write me soon is in Swedish "VAR SNALL OCH SKRIV SNART TILL MIG".

In another letter…

> Jag älskar dig, Sean (I write it in the air with a cigarette).

In another…

> I love you 50 X. The Swedish lesson for today is to learn how to spell to ten in Swedish. ETT, TVÅ, TRE, FYRA, FEM, SEX SJU, ÅTTA, NIO, TIO. Don't forget to learn it.

But one day, a shadow fell on the idyl.

It seems a Mr. A_____ had visited the cottage. He saw Agneta and decided that she would be an ideal girlfriend for his son. With luck the relationship would endure and the son would have a future wife. Nordic brides were in demand among the wealthy class of Toronto at that time. They were loyal, sensible, and produced tall blonde children. Most new relationships are threatened near the outset by a third party – it is a common plot complication in romance novels – and in this case the dark outsider was a grade above me at my high school.

Earlier, he'd visited the island briefly from a nearby cottage. Agneta reported the event indifferently, saying only that the visitor knew me. But suddenly...

"I have much to tell you but I want to write you. Yesterday Mr and Mrs A_____ came over for a drink on this island. And for some reason Mr A_____ asked me if I had got a letter from his son. I said yes. He was very concerned at me writing a letter to his son to cheer him up. Of course I didn't like that at all. Mr A_____ also asked the cottage owner's wife if she could not make me write a letter to his son. What could I do but write a letter to him? Now is everyone of their week end guests gone and the mother and I are alone with the two children. I'll write you again. This is my 14th letter I have written since I came to the island."

My response, unlike Agneta's, has not survived, but I must have been agitated because she writes later...

"You think that he is interested in me. I don't think he is as much as his father is concerned about me. I met Mr A_____ a few days ago and he asked me again if I had written to his son. I didn't answer him. Sean, you don't have to worie. I am still with you" (Monday the twentieth of August, 1960. Agneta's language quirks).

Apparently I took my confusion to Barbara, though I don't recall this; neither does she. But it provoked a defiant response from Agneta, who was more concerned that I had talked behind her back. A loyal, sensible companion.

The autumn after she came home, I felt a change. Not in her. The change was in me. For the first time, I realized Agneta was a beautiful young woman.

That long fall and winter we were together so much that it was simpler to include me in everything her family did. I ate *kräfton* or crayfish, an end-of-summer feast in Sweden with Schnapps and lager chasers. I learned how to make *glögg* — a spiced wine after-ski drink with candied orange peels, blanched almonds, cinnamon sticks, and cloves. "The key ingredient is this," her father said, stirring in a bottle of vodka. To my teenage eyes, Casten von Otter set a standard of cool never to be surpassed. He skied downhill smoking the butt of his cigar jammed in his pipe. He was photographed as a young cavalry officer in dress uniform going over a jump on a horse.

One evening at dinner, Mrs. Godfrey called. A Rosedale socialite, she was inclined to class attitudes and symbols. Agneta's father returned to the dinner table shaking his head. "She asked to speak to the Baron von Otter," he said. "I explained to her, I am not barren. Look! I have four daughters."

Four excited daughters talking all at once around the table, modulated by Vera von Otter, their mother, with the elegance of spirit of European aristocracy. And Ulla with the cheerful outlook of a camp counselor. She would soon marry her boyfriend Erik Sundström and become a Canadian citizen and live in Ajax, outside Toronto. And Caroline with her pre-teen conformity to social expectations and her astonishment at my suddenly answering her in Swedish. It was Caroline who recoiled from the hippie culture of Trent University. Diana, young and already beautiful. Barbara, always reserved and thoughtful.

Barbara at age thirteen already exhibited the signs of someone with a dynamic inner life. Later, she would remark that she regretted not becoming an academic. None of that showed in 1959. People, especially girls, weren't prized for their intellect during the insipid Fifties. Instead, the future Barbara showed in a quiet, insistent push for independence. As a grown-up woman she would later make her dad proud by becoming a member of parliament, an agent for a Swedish antiques firm, and the wife of an aristocrat, but at age thirteen her individuality irritated her father who was bothered by the self-possession of cats. So Barbara ran away from home. She ran west through the night, up to the railway tracks that bordered north Rosedale, then west across the bridge over a ravine to Summerhill Gardens.

I heard a tapping at my bedroom window. I can't remember what she said but it must have been about her father who was subject to displays of temper. In her urge to get away, she ran to the one place she knew she'd feel safe.

"But Agneta's going to phone any minute."

"Tell her I'm not here."

"She won't believe me."

"I'll be gone when she calls."

Barbara later
as Baroness Beck-Friis

She returned home. She had made her point. Her father relaxed. Some days later I heard him tell her, "As a father I'm not supposed to value any one of my children over another. But if I were to, I would value you the most."

Did he see himself in her?

After teenage, Agneta and I went separate ways as we began the adventure of growing up. I'd see her in a newspaper photo dressed as Saint Lucia with a circlet of tall white candles burning around her head, bringing light to the farmhouses and cattle stalls on the Winter Solstice. She was gone for awhile on the ski slopes of Europe. But she checked in when she returned — the beginning of a habit that arose whenever a current relationship was dubious. In the summer of 1967, she took a holiday from this and spent every Friday night with me. A decade and a half later when I had settled down, she arrived with her two children to see my new house and to meet Kelly whom she treated immediately as a friend. But there were problems in her own marriage; otherwise she wouldn't have come. I saw the problem for myself a few years later when I visited her home in a remote, time-locked place hacked out of the wilderness. Her flower garden encircling two sides of the house. A barn where her husband went to slaughter a chicken to roast for dinner, the act concluded with a shot of Polish vodka. Two Canadian children in a Middle European patriarchy.

And Barbara? She too plunged into the mayhem of the Sixties as traditional roles and expectations dissolved in existential relationships and one-night stands. I have a memory of her dashing out on a date, pausing beside the front drive to stuff lily of the valley down her bodice. She had a different appeal from that of her sister. She was more easily imaginable as a life mate. One aspiring suitor threatened to descend in a rented helicopter on the family ski cabin in Collingwood with a wedding ring. Expectations of absolute love ran up against the struggle to be your own person.

First love can be the one open-ended moment in their lives when two young people bring to their union all the relationships that go on in their families. And Agneta's was a big family. I was exposed to several human energies. There was the energy of father and daughter, of mother and daughter, of au pair to girls, of sister to sister. There was the all-transcending energy of husband and wife. And then the finer nuances of kinship in each of the four children, because the four girls were quite different. And my *ex officio* relationship, that of an older sister's fascinating boyfriend. Agneta played several roles. She could be big sisterly in her benign bossiness. She could be motherly. She could be ladylike, as on the Friday afternoons on the Park Plaza rooftop bar in 1967 when she wore a navy blue suit with earrings in the shape of tiny silver fish. She could be a wifely when that same year, walking all day from pavilion to pavilion at the Expo World Fair, she came back tired and excited to the apartment in Montreal rented by McClelland & Stewart.

I think of the counterpoint of family voices echoing in two people crossing the threshold from teenage into adulthood. That delicate, fugal kinship pre-empts the mechanisms of control asserted by one person over another. It endured across a lifetime.

Today, surveying a future marriage in a generation distant from mine, I feel like the elderly professor in Ingmar Berman's *Wild Strawberries*. He is searching for the meaning of his life in the past because he has little chance of finding it in the future. The Swedish title Bergman gave to his film is *Smultronstället*, literally, like a wild strawberry patch, a beautiful out-of-the-way place that has a special claim on the heart. The professor driving in a car into his past is an effigy of the guilt, introspection, and existential loneliness of Swedish puritanism. Jostling his way through visions and nightmares, he stumbles upon that special out-of-the-way place. It is a sign of redemption; of *his* redemption.

I was thirty-five years old when I found my lifelong partner. My car drive into the past, if I dared to go there, would be haunted by the reproachful ghosts of marital prospects. There was little wrong with them; only that they didn't fit the contours of the wild strawberry patch in my heart.

She died at her family home in Sweden. Every day during her last months, her mother left the house with the gold otters on the ceiling and walked down to spend the day with her first-born daughter in her cottage by the lake she knew as a girl. Barbara would visit her sister in hospital. Agneta took comfort from a framed picture on the far wall from her bed. Through all her suffering, her ambulance trips to Emergency, she never complained.

We are all swallowed by the Fengris wolf of time looming over the horizon. I dream of two sisters – one my first love; one a lifelong friend.

A between time

"Hell-lo!!!"
 "Hi! Got a minute?"
 "Sure. Lots of time."
 "Can you speak louder?"
 "*Is that better?*"
 "You sound like you're far away."
 "I'm … a little way away."
 "I thought you had a deadline for a conference paper."
 "I'm taking a break."
 "Just out of curiosity, where are you?"
 "I'm in Canmore. It's in the Rockies."
 "!"
 "Natasha took a break from work."
 Natasha's idea of relaxation is hiking the back slopes of well-known mountains whose rock faces claim the lives of experienced mountain-climbers. Owen does indoor climbing occasionally. I hope he isn't…
 "Don't worry. We're not doing the challenging stuff."
 "I had an idea about Shakespeare. But I guess this isn't the right time."
 "No, not really. We're on a stack looking out over a valley. It's really wide, and I think there's a river."
 Gulp! "Okay, call when you can. Don't take any risks."
 "We won't. Don't worry about us."

★ ★ ★

> *A between time; what's to come*
> *looms. Let it not loom.*
> *It has loomed enough.*
> *Let it, whatever it is, loom off.*
> — George Johnston

The in-between years — that chancy, haunted duration from retirement to death — haven't been fully imagined because there are better things for an elderly person to do than write books. We have a good idea of human nature at the other stages of life. Infancy and early childhood is thoroughly anticipated by motherlore and parenting books. Teenage is mapped by the media from pre-teen to young adult. Early adulthood and its drama of courtship is covered extensively in rom-com movies, sentimental fiction, and Broadway musicals. Advanced middle age has a voice in novels by Proust and Mann. But old age? Not very entertaining, apart from a few discouraging portraits like Shakespeare's *King Lear* and Margaret Laurence's *Stone Angel*. We can't imagine the inner life of the elderly, no way of knowing how to be old.

Until recently, the world hasn't known human longevity on a mass scale. In the 1920s, the life expectancy in my part of North America was 61. In 1950, it was 68.5. In 1966, it was 72. Much of the increase is due to huge reductions in infant and child mortality rates, but there have been gains at the upper end of the age range too. In 1920 a sixty-five-year-old man could expect to live another thirteen years. Ninety years later, that figure had increased to nineteen years — and of course a much higher proportion of the population now makes it to age sixty-five. Many people are living into their nineties. And my son's generation, the Millennials, may be the first generation to go off the actuarial charts altogether.

At the age of 102, William Blissett seems untroubled. He continues life on the uncertain plateau of retirement, attending Saint Mary Magdalene Church and researching at the Robarts Library.

He has been a parishioner of Saint Mary Magdalene since Ascension Day, 1945, when he says "the heavens opened" to the choir signing the Magnificat with antiphonal harmony from a second choir in a gallery at the back of the church. At Robarts, he has occupied the study carrel he was assigned the day the library opened in 1973. When he dies his carrel number should be retired. There is talk among the librarians of putting a plaque beside the carrel door.

That big question – what *is* to come? – evokes our incompleteness as human beings in the face of the unknown. The question is terrifying.

"Kel, what would you put in my obituary if I died suddenly?"

She says:

Sean Kane
1943 to 2025
He died from having lived.

"Is that all?

"What more is there to say?"

Time to change the topic.

A between time. I don't feel sandwiched – I feel hyphenated. I'm an inter-generational hyphen whose destiny is to mediate between wide-open behaviour and tiptoeing within the tolerances of society. But my generation of post-war Boomers was a long hyphen. Today's generation may find they are a short hyphen between aspiration and a fall from a great height.

6
THE DREAM OF BECOMING A WRITER

The first time I met Graeme Gibson, a bird was sitting on his shoulder. It was a full-grown parrot he'd brought from Mexico where he'd gone to write a novel. Harold Wilson lived for the times he could fly around the house shrieking; otherwise, he sat in his cage in the kitchen and looked out the window at Graeme's Jaguar sedan rusting in the backyard, and slowly went insane. His one diversion was calling Graeme in the voice of his wife Shirley, which he imitated perfectly. Graeme would be upstairs writing, and he'd hear her calling from the kitchen. *Grae-eme! Grae-eme!* He'd rush down to the kitchen to find Harold eyeing him with a coy slyness. This game couldn't go on – it was either the book or the bird. The Riverdale Zoo was glad to take the bird, and Graeme said goodbye without regret, placing Harold at the end of a long bar that ran the length of a cage. At the other end of the bar sat a wise and ancient female parrot. As Graeme turned and walked away, she began to inch down the bar towards Harold. That was when Graeme heard a sound that broke his heart.

Grae-eme! Grae-eme!

This masculinist vignette came into focus when I saw the narrative plan for his first novel, *Five Legs*, spread across his study wall. Everywhere was a motif of young men in states of mutilation. One was simply disemboweled. I identified this last figure as Adonis, the youthful dying god of classical mythology who fleeing voluptuous possession by Venus runs into a boar and is gored in the side, low enough to suggest sterility. Graeme had read Shakespeare's disturbing poem *Venus and Adonis*.

But in the plan on his wall, Adonis was linked with another young man in literature who dies before his time. This was Edward King, the fellow Cambridge student and poet who is the subject of the elegy *Lycidas* by John Milton. Graeme said it was his favourite poem. It suggested the dramatic situation of *Five Legs*. A professor is driving to the funeral of a promising young student who might have become a great novelist. He had died in a traffic accident on these same wintry Ontario roads. With the professor are the student's girlfriend and his close male friend, who has the unnerving silences in his personality that mark him as a writer too.

I don't know who taught *Lycidas* to Graeme, but whoever it was won a victory for creative writing not found anywhere else in his education. He repeated Grade One! How is it possible to fail Grade One? His high school years aren't notable, but they got him into officer training at the Collège Militaire Royale de Saint Jean. He dropped out after one year, though he enjoyed the experience of leadership, camaraderie, and the outdoors. Then to English and Philosophy at the University of Western Ontario, which he interrupted after second year to go to Edinburgh and find himself. Returning to Western, he failed his M.A., a feat he advertised proudly on the cover bio of his first novel. Throughout his entire formal education, no teacher picked up on the telltale signs of a young person harbouring a creative imagination.

This, in fact, was the third figure in the motif system that played out along Graeme's wall like the Bayeux Tapestry: the alienated creative youth fated to be overlooked, ignored, and ultimately failed by the system that chooses the elite for a narrow-minded, pragmatic society. Graeme would call him Felix. His prototype is Stephen Dedalus, the alter ego of a young James Joyce, escaping to Europe to become a Romantic artist in the face of a brutal, arid education. And also J.P. Donleavy's *Ginger Man* with its wasted, lecherous hero blowing his American father's allowance on a failed education at Trinity College Dublin.

Graeme saw in the creative writer a complex psychology. Such people have a visionary imagination, allowing them to x-ray the habits and customs of their society. People who live in their head are a bore, especially in formal settings requiring insincere expressions of sentiment, such as a funeral. You never know what maladroit observation the repressed creative soul is likely to blurt out next. And they seem always on the edge of taking flight.

In the funeral scene of *Five Legs*, the silently observing Felix is a spirit inhabiting a body. But that's not unusual if you know Gibson's writing. He doesn't write about flesh-bound people; he writes about their thought-streams. Their mental events have a tendency to become real, as when Felix, now trying to survive in Graeme's second novel, *Communion*, sees two stone angels on a tombstone shedding actual tears. In *Five Legs*, Felix's right arm detaches during a hearty Rotarian handshake at the reception following the funeral. "Give me back my arm!" he says matter-of-factly. But what is truly scary is the deceased youth's mother descending on him with a corpulent sensuality. His classmate must have been fleeing from the daughter of this matriarchal Venus when he drove his car into a truck. The girlfriend, weakened by the English professor's flattering attention, is discovered upstairs with the professor on the deceased's bed in his bedroom, now turned into a memorial shrine. Felix's reaction? He breaks into giddy laughter. In *Communion*, Felix finds himself in a room full of drunk women. One of them asks him what he does best. He points to the back door and says: "When it's absolutely essential, I can walk from here to there."

When *Five Legs* was published in 1969, most readers interpreted the condition troubling Felix as the Protestant work ethic. That was how Scott Symons, then a voice against sexual repression, described the book in a front-cover quote. The interpretation suited a time when the work ethic was enemy to every suburban child with a free spirit. Graeme was alert to that ethic in its earlier nineteenth-century form as a down-to-earth pioneering labour that didn't tolerate the frivolity of art. It squelched the artistic joy in the prairie wife of Sinclair Ross's *As For Me and My House*, a Canadian classic that may have inspired Graeme – he later made it into a film script. Born in London, Ontario, an epicentre of Scottish-Canadian rural culture, Gibson is the inventor of the literary style known as "Ontario Gothic," though Alice Munro is its best practitioner.

But Gibson went deeper than capturing a period style. He was driven to expose the source of this death-dealing psychology in Western thought. His mission was confirmed when he went to the office of Professor Carl Klinck, seeking a thesis topic that suited his interest in the figure of the emerging modern novelist. A one-man CanLit industry, Klinck had catapulted from course instructor to full professor in four years, skipping the ranks in between. He opened the drawer of an elongated metal case for holding index cards – the 3 × 5 inch ruled cards used for research in those days. Flicking through them, he extracted a card and handed it to Graeme, like a doctor giving a prescription. Graeme stared at the topic.

Morley Callaghan and the Smart Set

He left the office puzzled. He knew who Morley Callaghan was. Everybody did. Active since the 1920s when he met fellow journalist Ernest Hemingway at the *Toronto Star*, and mixing briefly with the Lost Generation writers in Paris, Callaghan was still writing his spare, precise moral novels in the 1960s. *The Smart Set* turned out to be a New York society magazine fashionable in the Twenties when it published extracts by new writers. But the support of a milieu of fellow writers made no sense to Gibson, who at that time in his life was an outsider.

Years later, in the early Seventies while having coffee at Wymilwood in Victoria College, I met a graduate student fresh from Western and eager to talk about CanLit.

"Did you work with Carl Klinck?"

"Of course. Everyone does."

"Did he stick you with *Morley Callaghan and the Smart Set*?"

"???!!! How do you know that?"

Graeme told me he subsequently met Callaghan at a party. He shared the fact that he once intended to research the novelist's relationship with *The Smart Set*.

"Oh, that old thing!" Callaghan said.

Analysing the existential threat to a writer doesn't come easily to someone who is caught in the condition. Graeme told Eugene Benson, his friend at Western, that he spent ten or fifteen years in "contemplation" for his first novel. The term is from the social philosopher George Grant and it means thinking within the Western tradition of thought going back to Plato. The motifs I saw on Graeme's wall date from at least 1956–7 when, reacting to turbulent world events, he began a journal and toyed with becoming a journalist. Edinburgh scenes from that year feature in Felix's stream-of-consciousness which takes up the second half of *Five Legs*. Graeme worked further on his novel between late 1959 and the spring of 1961 when he left London, Ontario – where he had just failed his M.A. – for London, England, taking with him Shirley Warrington, a married woman from Western's artistic subculture. Shirley and Graeme would have their first son Matthew during an exile that roamed from the front room of a Battersea bedsit to the rent-free use of a house on the Point d'Antibe on the French Riviera. In 1964–5, they lived in the house in Oaxaca that Frieda and D.H. Lawrence had occupied, Graeme drinking mescal in the town square as the novelist Malcolm Lowry had done.

This all seemed very romantic to me, an impressionable graduate English student. Imagine selling your family home in Rosedale to finance a quest for authentic existence as a writer. What impresses me today as I recall this history is that Graeme didn't simply act out the twentieth-century norm of expatriate writer leaving North America for the stimulation of an artistic milieu. He was already stimulated. He didn't need a milieu. He needed to get a story off his chest. That story happened in his final year at Western and may have been the whole reason for his becoming a novelist.

Now, Gibson is living on the French Riviera with Shirley and their recently born son Matthew. In a fragile state, he opens a registered package containing his first novel in draft and a commentary by Gene Benson. His eyes fall on the first sentence: "I have many doubts about the structure of your novel." He darts to the end of the letter to read the summation: "What does Wally Ryerson [the actual fellow student who died in a traffic accident] and S. Ontario and Western U. and the life you lived and your deepest emotions mean to *you*?"

Eugene Benson, the author of this risky letter, is a multifarious genius in an ongoing state of harmony. He greets you in the lobby of his condominium complex on Toronto's Beaches, wearing a cravat under a white jersey, creased trousers, and stylish shoes. This man has known many worlds. He could be a successful playwright, a music festival director, a librettist for operas, a novelist, a yachtsman on the Aegean, an executive of PEN Canada, the president of the Writers Union of Canada, a senior academic. In fact, Gene has been all of these. One vocation that didn't pan out was Missionary Catholic priest trained in the Jesuit Order. Another was member of parliament for the Ontario NDP. Both long shots. At the time of writing the letter to Graeme he was teaching English at Royal Military College on a temporary appointment. Back to the letter:

> Line of Story: I don't know where your story is going…
> Tone of Prose: Not good enough … drab and pedestrian…
> Character (psychology) analysis: Each character must reveal a distinctive … prose idiom…
> Allusion … leit motif: …Why not take some poem … and use that as a device in the way Joyce used Homer?… Milton's *Lycidas* (?). But note Joyce used this in Ulysses…"

The letter goes on, critical and uncompromising. At its midway point, it offers consolation: "I am sure you must, Graeme, be apoplectic by this time at this re-writing of your novel." But "my only excuse for being so cavalier is that I feel you are constipated…" Benson then issues the strategic correctives, a hand to a drowning man. This certainly puts a writer at a crux. Then the final summation:

> Report: Can you write? I don't know. Maybe you can and maybe you can't. Too many censors are operating… Beat your head against a wall a few times to loosen up; dig into your psyche; use music, drink, prayer, love…

Graeme's reaction? He wrote Gene immediately, saying "It pleased me that you have taken me to task for this, that your letter truly rocked me as it did, for I had in my perverse way felt I would have to leave this to another book…"

Benson wrote Gibson a prescription for how to become a writer. And Gibson followed it to the letter, though in his own good time. It would be eight years until *Five Legs* was published. Stubbornly, it had the same theme and characters as the original draft he entrusted to Benson. Forty-five years later, he would tell an audience to his Margaret Laurence Lecture: "Despite dismay and spasms of self-pity, I was oddly comforted that Eugene's judgments hadn't surprised me, that – not for the first time in my life – I'd been fooling myself. In the event I returned earnestly to his letter… [Y]ears later I pulled out his letter and that first desperate text and confirmed how fair and constructive Eugene had been. To this day I consider his among the most courageous and valuable gifts I have received as a writer."

It is a sign of Graeme's integrity that *Five Legs* survived this edit. Just as it is a sign of his integrity when he earlier pitched a novel written in Edinburgh over the stern of the ship taking him back to Canada. "A man of genius makes no mistakes. His errors are volitional and are the portals to discovery," James Joyce says through his alter ego Stephen Dedalus.

It was 1965 when I came across Graeme and Shirley. It was rumoured that, as well as a parrot, he had brought a young Mexican woman to help with the household – they had two sons now. Far from home the poor woman was in a state of terror. We connected Graeme with Dr. John Rich, a member of the Rosedale NDP and a noted child psychiatrist. The distressed woman returned to Mexico safely. Her place in the attic apartment of the rented house was taken by Jane Barnett, a B.A. student in English at Victoria College. We would sit together in the kitchen under a potted avocado tree while Graeme made mixed bean salad and recounted the day's epiphany. Walking through an early morning mist in the adjacent park, he saw a line of bent-over trolls, each with a single eye in the middle of its forehead, lurching toward him. It was clear by the intensity with which he told it, his eyes widening, arms waving, that this gothic moment had a place in his novel. It entered the manuscript as a hallucination experienced by Felix in the graveyard following the funeral service. (The line of men bent over buckets strapped to their legs were actually Portuguese worm-pickers.) Jane herself entered *Five Legs* as another nurse motif, her maternal instinct fastened to a dog named Queenie she took for walks. The dog had five legs. (The real Queenie was a perfectly normal Alsatian who belonged to a neighbour up the street.) I think I'm in the novel too, condensed into the figure of the creative spirit facing a choice at university: study literature or write it.

For I was like Graeme. I had also lost my mother when I was young, and I also was sent to Upper Canada College. I too lived in my father's shadow – though not like Graeme whose father was the youngest Brigadier in the Canadian Army in Holland in 1945. Judging by Felix's chronic behaviour, Graeme sought his missing mother in young women, putting himself in the contradiction of rejecting a comfort he was obsessively drawn to. Yet he saw how this need to "hold me tight and set me free" infantilizes men and makes women old before their time. Shakespeare's *Venus and Adonis* provided the archetype. Recounting the poem to me, he focused on a drop of perspiration on Venus's body. The overheated sensuality of the love goddess as she mothers an Adonis seeking his freedom to create. Allegorical commentary in Shakespeare's time saw the myth as a parable of the creative process – the universal process of creating life through the joining of the seed to matter. The flighty imperishable seed or form is Adonis; matter (Latin: *mater*), restlessly, changing its appearance to accommodate the form, is Venus. I regret I didn't take Graeme's central symbol to heart at the time. Graeme didn't either, remaining throughout his life an allure to women.

The myth allowed him to use the High Modernist technique of the *leitmotif* or repeated image to expose what he saw as the defining feature of modernity. The defining feature is the *denial of the immediacy of experience*. Instead of being felt fully in the senses, experience is negotiated at second hand by the intellect. This impulse goes back to Plato's elevation of reason for the project of managing the Earth. Graeme saw its cost in the sterility of the male artist and the unfulfilled sensuality of the woman. Inspired by the Polish writer Jerzy Kosiński, he would go on to explore this paradigm in *Communion*. Now the tormented Felix shuttles between a wife and a mistress. The two are separated by Toronto's Don Valley which offers him the temporary solace of wilderness. Felix embodies the fatal result of denying the senses: the management of the world through technology. The book was written in 1969 and 1970, and reflects that era when peasant villages in Vietnam were bombed with a jellied gasoline called napalm and cities in America burned during the race riots. The period song "Children of Darkness" – sung by Joan Baez and Mimi Fariña and written by Baez's brother-in-law Richard Fariña before he died in a motorcycle accident – is also very much of this time, with its references to "the light of reason" failing as "fires burn on the sea." As for Felix, he catches fire and disappears in flames on the Rainbow Bridge as he draws closer to the U.S. from Canada.

Gibson set his third novel, *Perpetual Motion*, in a recollection of the pioneer life that coloured Canadian nationalism during the Seventies. Here, the mission to dominate the Earth rationally is displayed in the protagonist's constructing a machine that will generate its own power infinitely. The nightmare accompanying this contradiction is the slaughter to extinction of the Carrier Pigeons that once darkened the sky during migration. Elsewhere in the book, intimate human relationships with others including wild birds and animals are destroyed by technological modernity.

In relation to the vulnerable male writer, Graeme's fourth novel, *Gentleman Death*, is interesting because it is the most personal. The Gibson alter ego, the maimed blocked novelist, says goodbye to his dying brother in London, then to recover the balancing principle of love elaborates a fictional scenario about finding his Scottish roots in a smoky Hebrides bar with a spirited Highland woman. It doesn't work. She dies from cancer. In a second speculative fantasy, set in Berlin, he meets a woman who like the first might have offered the comfort of love together with a nobility of spirit, if he had pursued these what if's. Back in Toronto with his sensible partner, he deals with his father, now hallucinating in a state of senility, and with an incomprehensible new generation heralded by his precocious daughter.

My time at Graeme and Shirley's home during my graduate school years was transformational. There were two young boys, Matthew and Grae, brought up with devotion (today's enlightened parenting wasn't the norm then). They weren't my anti-family, but they were a walk away on Rosehill Avenue across the park from Summerhill Gardens where I lived. We talked about new books: the love somehow pushing through the mechanization of instinct in Cohen's *Beautiful Losers*; the echoes of *The Waste Land* in Bob

Dylan's "Desolation Row." The violence of the late Sixties spilled out of Graeme's television set. I watched the 1968 Democratic Party Convention with him, when the delegates had to settle for a career politician following the assassination of the idealistic Robert Kennedy. The mayor of Chicago, an old-style ward politician, released the police force on thousands of demonstrators while the betrayed convention delegates chanted, *"The whole world is watching."* That year, Graeme, whose attitude to American dominance had reached an all-time low, found a cop on either side of him at La Guardia Airport in New York. They hustled him into the interrogation room. "So, what do you do for a living?" the senior officer asked him. "I'm a novelist." "Hey! this guy says he's a novelist," the officer said, and authorized a strip search. Yet it was Graeme who managed the immediate release of a drunken friend from police custody by assuming his military manner and demanding, "What seems to be the problem here, sergeant?"

For relief, there was touch football on Sunday mornings with the ornithologist and wildlife philosopher Jack Livingston, who Graeme considered one of the four influential Canadian thinkers of his generation along with Marshall McLuhan, Northrop Frye, and George Grant. Then Friday afternoons on the Park Plaza roof bar after a week teaching his course "Introduction to Despair" to nurses and secretaries at Ryerson Institute of Technology (now Toronto Metropolitan University). Having learned how to penetrate the defenses put up by indifferent students in a tough school in London, Graeme went straight to the core of a work. Could Frost's "the woods are lovely, dark and deep" be a death wish? Did Prufrock realize he was a poet without imagination? In my M.A. year, Graeme taught me the imperative that had sabotaged his own M.A.: put the imagination at the centre of your life and never unknowingly play a part in someone else's agenda.

Much of my education on the Park Plaza roof that summer came from Graeme's colleagues at Ryerson: Eric Wright and Bob Rodg-

Graeme Gibson teaching his "Introduction to Despair"
course at Ryerson in the mid-1960s
*(Harold Barkley/*Toronto Star*)*

ers, and their wives, Valerie and Sylvia, who ran a fashionable stocking shop in Yorkville called *Gambit*. Eric Wright would emerge as a popular murder mystery author. Bob Rogers turned his creativity to the U of T film centre, which probably cost him the novel he was only able to write at the end of his life. Agneta, drinking Campari and soda beside me, laughed with Bob's story of the time a U of T friend, Brian Summerhayes, went to the office of Professor Douglas Grant to get out of writing an essay on eighteenth-century literature. "I don't want to write on Jane Austen," he said. "I want to write about Ernest Hemingway." Grant had been a Royal Marine Commando in World War Two. He looked across his desk with a level gaze at Summerhayes: "Do you realize I could kill you with one blow?"

After the Park Plaza roof, we would go, the eight of us, to a romantic Hungarian restaurant where the violinist on seeing him enter broke into Graeme's favourite piece. Once at Agneta's invitation, we moved the party to her parent's house and swam in the swimming pool surrounded by her favourite yellow roses.

Graeme finished *Five Legs* on August 12, 1967, after seven years of hitting each word with a tuning fork to make sure it resonated. I sent him across the park to my father in Summerhill Gardens. Graeme had the most capacious unconscious of any novelist I have met: he could talk all day about the modern novel in Argentina, in Turkey, in Czechoslovakia, in every country this art form was practiced. After an afternoon drinking whiskey and hearing him describe the art of the novel, my father, soon to be president of Macmillan of Canada, was ready to publish him on the spot. The manuscript was absorbed into the turmoil that was "McStew" at the time, to be personally rejected five months later in Graeme's presence by Jack McClelland during a profile interview for *Time* magazine on the Park Plaza roof bar. Graeme harboured this slight in his long Celtic memory, along with his failed M.A. at the hands of the English professor at Western.

Eventually, Graeme was directed to Dennis Lee at the new House of Anansi Press. Lee recognized the submission to be the first modernist novel in Canada, barring Sheila Watson's experimental *The Double Hook* in 1949. *Five Legs* had a successful commercial sale for a complex stream-of-consciousness novel, largely on the strength of a

Dennis Lee at his home on Shaftesbury Avenue in the summer of 1973. "So the first time I met Dennis... Perhaps he was changing his storm windows... Could he have been washing windows? I was standing with the MS of *Five Legs*, which he'd agreed to consider for the House of Anansi, a publisher I hadn't even heard of a month before." – Graeme Gibson

weekend *Globe and Mail* review titled "A Glowing Anti-Puritanism in Sorrow." At the launching party, held in the studio apartment I shared with a draft-dodger, the management tried to end the event by shutting off the water. It was Graeme who kept the party going

Graeme Gibson, Shirley, and Grae

long into the night by periodically transferring ice water from the bathtub, where it cooled the beer, to the toilet. This was typical of Graeme whose social ebullience came from his mother, a radio entertainer. He handled every social crisis with generosity and resourcefulness. At a large dinner party at his house, someone brought a lurking depression to the table. So pervasive was the mood that its source couldn't be located. It silenced talk altogether. Graeme gave out pots and pans, instructing us to bang them with spoons in time to Mexican music. It worked: the vexed spirit left the room.

I saw less of Graeme after *Five Legs* was published. At a family outing at the farm of a friend of mine with a swimming pool, it was clear his marriage was breaking down. In this disordered state, Graeme and Shirley plunged into small press publishing at Anansi in the heyday of cultural nationalism.

About that time Graeme met Margaret Atwood, putting together *Survival*, her textbook for the new CanLit. Discovering the mystery of direct experience in bird-watching, they began to sponsor trips to wilderness places in Central America and the Arctic. My most enduring vision of Graeme as a leader happened on the last night of a bird-watching expedition around the Bay of Pigs area of Cuba. We were sitting in the departure lounge of a small airport waiting for a plane to take us home. I had lost the sole of my right running shoe – it lay in the sucking mud of a swamp where we'd been searching for the Bachman's Warbler, thought to have become extinct during a hurricane.

Bird-watching in the aptly named Zapata swamp

Graeme was wearing his British army bush jacket with a binocular case and ammunition pockets swelling with dubious packages (actually, penicillin kits to treat infected saw-grass lesions). His skin was brown from the tropical sun; he wore a red bandana around his neck. It was 4:00 in the morning in January of 1987 (Margaret Laurence had just died). A battalion of Cuban infantry in full military gear sat in rows across the aisle from us. They were flying secretly to Nicaragua by night to evade CIA surveillance. Each group examined the other silently: the bird-watchers and the soldiers, both dressed for the jungle.

Graeme separated himself from his ragtag squadron of bird-watchers and strode down the length of the aisle in front of the soldiers, his back ramrod-straight and his moustache drooping like a Spanish-American guerilla leader. ¿Who is this *hombre*? ¿One of the original 26 July movement revolutionaries? ¿A friend of Fidel's? All along the rows, the soldiers stiffened to attention as Graeme went by.

Graeme, aware of the reaction he provoked, was delighted. He admired the visionary leader of Cuban socialism. It was Fidel Castro who entering Havana on January 8, 1959, looked out over the masses of people gathered to hear him speak. At that moment, a dove flew down and sat on his shoulder.

A sacred trust

"I will not cease from Mental Fight ..."

People are getting to their feet. The speaker is rising to a triumphant affirmation. He's evangelic – literally, a messenger bringing the good news.

"Nor shall my Sword sleep in my hand ..."

The quote: that's William Blake. It became the hymn of the British Labour Party. Thousands of party supporters sang it victoriously in Trafalgar Square on the night of the great election of 1945 which brought in the National Health Service. The Labour government accomplished a lot for post-war Britain but nothing they did addressed human suffering more directly than the NHS.

And here in Ottawa in 1961, T.C. Douglas is dedicating himself to Medicare. Tommy Douglas who as Premier of Saskatchewan introduced a public health plan for seniors two years after the British Labour victory. Now he's going to bring it to Canada as leader of a New Democratic Party at its founding convention. Delegates from across Canada – trade unionists, farmers, shop workers, teachers, nurses – begin to cheer.

"'Til we have built Je-ru-sa-lem ..."

Tommy's voice rises above the sustained cheering. There's a note of prophetic fulfillment. The Gaelic care to pronounce each syllable. For the next seven years he'll say *Med-ee-care* in the House of

Tommy Douglas at the founding convention
of the New Democratic Party
(Duncan Cameron/Library and Archives Canada)

Commons until a Liberal government can't stand listening to him anymore and introduces the legislation. They introduce it on Tommy Douglas's terms without watering it down because the restless, brooding social conscience across the aisle won't let them off the hook of a minority government. Medicare will become national (a federal responsibility), universal (for every Canadian regardless of income), and accountable (funding will be witheld if any doctor, clinic, hospital, or provincial government charges a profit). Thus a public trust is protected. This was the model introduced in Saskatchewan. Soon after, a Conservative Prime Minister confirmed the model by offering funding on a 50-50 basis to any province that followed it. The 50 percent portion gave Ottawa leverage against any provincial impulse to make a profit on human suffering. The principle of a universal public plan was unequalled in the democratic world. Even Great Britain weakened and allowed two tier medicine.

"In this our green and pleasant Land."

But the last line with its reverential falling cadence is drowned out by the sustained cheering. A new party, the NDP, has been born and has received its mandate.

I was just back from visiting Agneta at her summer home in Sweden. Her background complemented my last school year on the fringes of the Toronto high-school U.N. networks where some students were setting up New Democratic Party Clubs. The riding of Peterborough had already elected a New Democratic Party member to parliament. So going to Sweden, I kept my eyes open. It had enjoyed the fruits of social democracy continuously since the 1920s. An ancestor of Agneta's, Prime Minister Fredrik Wilhelm von Otter, introduced progressive taxation and universal suffrage at the turn of the century.

Social democracy fit the Swedish national character. In Stockholm, a pair of police officers carrying ceremonial swords saluted me when I approached to ask for directions. Can you imagine a cop saluting you in North America? Everything seemed courteous and sensible, including the politics. At a restaurant on the highway – we'd call it a truck stop – I turned to go into the room with the starched table cloths, silverware, and elegant glasses. But no. That wasn't for ordinary motorists; that was for the transport truck drivers. A perk negotiated by their union.

But the major foundation of the national purpose I discovered in Sweden wasn't the nationalized all-electric railway system or the scrupulous neutrality in world affairs, but the fact that Sweden had developed its own industrial base. Think Volvo, Electrolux, IKEA, Saab, ABBA. Private enterprise generated the wealth that paid for the social benefits. Canada couldn't maintain its own industrial base because of the pressure to sell to American interests. It was easier to rely on the American economy to create our wealth for us. "Americans like to make money. Canadians like to count it. I know of no other country where the accountant is held in such high esteem." This is Northrop Frye, who taught me Blake. He refused offers of an endowed chair at American universities because of two unique Canadian institutions: the United Church of Canada and the NDP.

Medicare was an instant hit. People no longer had to go bankrupt to pay for complex surgery. They didn't have to save up to see a family doctor. Medicare held the country together better than the NHL. Whether they voted, Conservative, Liberal, or NDP, people believed in a universal national health plan. In a CBC poll, Tommy Douglas was voted the most significant figure in Canada's history. Brian Mulroney, a Conservative and the last of Canada's aspirational prime ministers, called Medicare "a sacred trust." Of course, private profit soon began nibbling around the edges. Quebec was the first to allow individuals to jump to the front of the line for an MRI if they paid extra. A medical victim using the B.C. public ambulance service had to pay cost-recovery based on the length of the trip. The government of New Brunswick held discussions with an American hospital management corporation. But the core principle of Medicare prevailed against constant lobbying by U.S. life insurance companies and drug corporations. Medicare remained a universal, single-user system. The key to its success, the lynchpin of the whole system, was funding by the federal government.

Then a Liberal government in Ottawa cut the provincial funding transfer. Provinces passed the funding cut down to the municipalities, and the downtown streets were sprinkled with homeless, sick, addicted, and mentally unstable people. The central principle of a national health plan was shaken. Yet the federal government still held onto enough of their percentage contribution to control profiteering. Then came the pandemic of 2020.

Provincial governments adapted variously to the stress this put on Medicare. The Conservative government of Ontario, which had already frozen nurses' salaries along with those of the rest of the public sector, saw an opportunity to turn over certain elective surgeries to private medical corporations. The New Democrat government in British Columbia did the opposite: surgeries actually increased during Covid; the number of nurses was tripled; a nursing program was started at Simon Fraser University; doctors were freed of the troublesome per-service system of compensation; the salaries of hospital and ambulance workers were increased; the province began to roll back for-profit clinics.

And Ottawa? It followed its earlier tactic with the pandemic when masking became controversial. The prime minister, who had appeared daily on the steps of his residence to demonstrate leadership in a pandemic crisis, disappeared from view. The chief medical officer of Canada with her gentle, trustworthy intelligence disappeared with him. Suddenly, Medicare belonged to the provinces. Canada no longer had one universal plan but ten separate plans, plus plans for Yukon and the Territories and for the First Nations. The horses of privatized medicine were out of the stable.

Today I am staring at a headline: "Medical Clinic to Open in Walmart." I'm afraid to read the story: "The Peterborough store [will be] one of more than 75 Walmart locations across Canada to include a Jack Nathan Health medical clinic on-site." And "Unlike most family practices, in addition to seeing registered patients for scheduled health appointments, Jack Nathan Health Clinics are also open to walk-in patients during clinic hours." Who is Jack Nathan? It doesn't say. Without checking further, my guess is that he is an American entrepreneur, probably once a doctor like Glenn Copeland, president and CEO of Jack Nathan Medical Inc. The staff at these clinics will be nurse practitioners lured from public health by bigger salaries and regular working hours. Recruiters have been said to be waiting for them in hospital parking lots after they come off shift, tired and underpaid. And I discovered that the Ontario Conservative government pays a privately owned clinic more than twice what it pays the public hospitals to do the same operation: $1264 (private) versus $508 (public) for cataract surgery; $4637 (private) versus $1273 to $1692 (public) for knee meniscus repair.

As I write this today, it is not impossible to return to universal, public, not-for-profit Medicare.

7
THE DREAM OF MEDICARE

A glorious June Day for Trent's outdoor convocation! Motorcycle traffic across the river has been stilled. The parents have been given their complimentary water bottles. Colin Campbell, who traditionally leads the parade of graduands with his bagpipes, is true to form. And an array of faculty in colourful robes from their original universities are present, including me wearing my University of Toronto doctoral gown. I had no inkling that by the end of the day I'd be flat out in intensive care, constantly watched by a nurse.

The day went without glitches. The chancellor, a CBC actor and Indigenous spiritualist, gave each and every graduate an intimate, heartfelt message of inspiration, translating convocation into

Owen Kane receiving the B.A., congratulated by Trent's founding president Tom Symons

a succession of individual life moments. There was no awkwardness about a student's degree being witheld because of an unpaid library fine, unlike my Toronto convocation where after the chancellor's *admitto te ad gradum* the student passed through a door under the stands to be greeted by the University Accountant with a ledger. On the far side of his table were all the nicely framed degrees. But at Trent there was no smallmindedness. It hosted a splendid reception in the echoing stone Great Hall with its line of doors open on the river side so parents could take photographs on the lawn.

I felt good about everything. Owen would be staying for another two years studying for an M.A. in Theory, Culture, and Politics, with his thesis supervised by Tom Symons. They would meet weekly around his fireplace and Tom would hand on his knowledge of Canada's unique history, together with the civility he exuded. I wonder what he'll make of Owen's current fascination with Nietzsche.

Convocations are rites of passage. They originally marked a candidate's fitness to join a select guild of people devoted to working in a branch of knowledge. At the first European universities, the novice received a bell, a book, and a candle to symbolize their future preoccupation. In some, they received a sword, the life of the mind being a virtuous discipline akin to chivalry. Today, convocations are a maturity ritual marking the candidate's fitness for marriage and employment. Content that Owen's transition into higher learning was formalized, I went home to relax while he partied with his classmates.

Around nine that night, writing a letter at my desk, I feel something isn't right.

"Kel, I'm feeling like shit."

"Do you mean queasy?"

"Yes, that's it. Queasy."

"Are you going to faint?"
"Maybe ... can't be sure."
"Do you want to throw up?"
"No. But I need a Tums."
"Point to the pain."
"There."

"Sub-sternal." She feels my brow. "Clammy. You're sweating, but no temperature. Let's go to Emerg. Where's your OHIP card?"

Twelve minutes later, a triage nurse asks me the same questions. But instead of *queasy* she asks about a *burning sensation*.

"Yes. I have a burning sensation. It's sub-sternal."

The nurse sits up straight. She takes my pulse at the wrist. Cold, gentle hand.

Then blood pressure. "Any allergies? No? Good. Would you come with me, please?"

I'm in a curtained alcove off Triage with bright lights, a gurney, and a row of taps for gas. "Hey, let's snort some oxygen."

"Stop fooling around," Kel says.

A motherly woman appears with a cart holding equipment for an electrocardiogram. She isn't rushed, she's relaxed and chatty but she works efficiently. She takes a strip of paper from the machine, glances at it, and leaves the room.

The triage nurse appears. "Would you like to follow me?" I follow her along a series of red arrows through a door into Emerg proper, then into another alcove like the first, except it has a freshly made bed with clean sheets. Oh, I'd really like to sleep right now. I feel...

There's no death experience, folks. No bright lights and distant music. It's just lights out.

It looks like anterior RVA. Sending the ECG up to you now. Click of a phone handset replaced on its bracket.

Spirit beings are sticking things on me. An angel is trying to tug my pants off.

Let Colleen do it. She can get the pants off anybody.

Damp with urine, the pants are handed at arm's length to Kelly.

He's waking up.

An angel on my left is adjusting a tube that's feeding immortality elixir into my arm. Another angel beside her is wiping her hands. Two more of them on the right side of my bed are frowning critically. Am I fit to graduate into heaven? I can't graduate. I haven't paid my library fine. I close my eyes and go inward for safety.

How are you feeling?

How am I feeling? I'm feeling like roadkill on the River Road that's just been run over by the Peterborough chapter of Hell's Angels playing bagpipes.

Are you feeling pain anywhere?

That is an intriguing, interesting question. I turn it over in my mind. My mind is the one part of me that feels okay. Not just okay, it has a never experienced such lucidity.

I said, do you feel any pain?

"Oh, sorry. I feel a distant sensation of pain but it's not worth elaborating. It is probably a body memory left over from my past existence when I had to pay a library fine in order to become a Doctor of Philosophy. In any case, it's post-critical, if you know what I mean. It's the kind of pain that indicates something *has* happened, not something is happening now or for that matter will happen in the immediate future."

On a scale of one to ten, ten being the worst pain you've ever known, what number would you give your pain?

This is worth further reflection. I've never experienced the pain of gallstones, pancreatitis, childbirth, deep muscle spasm, bone break. Presumably, those are tens. In fact, there is no reference point for my pain except listening to a politician explaining how carbon trapping will solve global warming. I have lived a pain-free existence.

The question again: *What number would you give your pain?* This comes from the middle angel on the right who wears glasses. An angel wearing glasses? I need to take this mask off.

No, leave it on, please.

"I've been giving some thought to your question."

And?

"I think perhaps 'two.' Because it's a dull pain around my chest, not a sharp focussed pain one might identify as internal. The sensation is like getting punched in the chest, not that I've ever been in a fight…"

A soft whisper. *It's the oxygen doing this.*

"Would the physician come forward?" I ask. My head is still full of ceremony from the morning's event. He's at the foot of the bed typing notes on an iPad. It will turn out years later when I peeked at my hospital medical file that every person at my bedside that day filed a report on the event.

"You had a heart attack," the doctor states matter-of-factly.

"I have some questions. First, I…"

"The team is on their way from the Cath Lab. They're taking over."

Cath Lab? What's a Cath Lab? Oh, there's Kel. She's come back from somewhere. A surgeon appears with two lean, athletic surgical nurses. He's holding a print-out. "See that? That's a blocked artery. We're going to open it up, with your permission."

I stare at the place where the heart rhythm went haywire. It looks like a dense up-and-down scrawl, as if the heart lost it and threw a tantrum. "An operation?"

"I'm going to look around. Check the condition of the other arteries in your heart. Then, I'll put in a stent. I need to tell you there is a risk, as there is with any surgery. Cardiac stenting is 95 percent successful. Would you sign the consent form?"

Gulp! 95 percent means one out of twenty operations is a failure. I could be the one out of twenty. The consent form is under my nose on a clipboard. I sense a gentle urgency. Dr. Ho leans over to see if my signature is shaky.

"No cognitive deficits," I announce brightly.

The surgical team take over the gurney, a nurse at each end. Just before I exit the alcove, one of the Emerg nurses calls, "Good luck!"

Then Owen appears. He must have broken a speeding bylaw to get here so fast. Kel had called him while she was out of the room. More time has passed than I estimate.

As I process by, his eyes meet mine. He has something to say. Something important. Something supportive. He leans over and says: "Remember Nietszche: *Anything that doesn't kill you will make you stronger.*"

This is something like what heart attacks were like in the early days of emergency stenting. I remember the catheter punching into the artery at the left groin. The X-ray machine whirring overhead on its rail and pausing, showing where the doctor was focused. No chatter, only hushed commands. And my mood? Even before the Ativan injection, I achieved the state of pure detachment the Buddha found underneath the Bo tree. Nothing mattered. Nothing mattered at all. It was all the same to me whether I lived or died. From the cath lab, I floated in a trance to the ICU to be hooked into equipment that monitored my heartbeat and blood pressure. An angel watched me constantly through a small window at the corner of my room. She assessed the quality of perfusion, the degree to which the arteries in the heart were becoming saturated with oxygen-bearing blood. She checked as my heart hunted for and eventually recovered its original rhythm. When Kel and Owen arrived after a briefing from Dr. Ho, they told me he'd put one stent in the right ventricular artery. The pacemaking cells in the heart wall hadn't diminished in number to a point where I would notice anything different.

After they left I spent the first night with that silent nurse watching over me. Nurses hold the world together. I believe every nurse in Canada who worked on the front line during the respiratory virus pandemic of 2020 should be given the Order of Canada. On the day of Owen's coming-of-age and my own near graduation from life, a thread of mortality held us.

Literary studies today

Riiiiing! Riiiiing!
"Hi!"
"Hi. Where are you?"
"I'm at the airport. I'm waiting for a flight."
"Flight? What flight?"
"To London. For the Shakespeare and the Sea conference."
"Yes, of course. At Greenwich. Is your paper ready to go?"
"I've got … a little work to do over Iceland."
"Once, after a Plenary Lecture, we insisted that future guest speakers travel by boat."
"I think better on a plane. The sensation of a rapidly approaching deadline concentrates the mind wonderfully."

How many wonderful talks we've had, boosted by espresso, striking sparks, making discoveries. "Have a look around the old Naval College. Christopher Wren designed it. You can see the actual line marking Greenwich Mean Time. If you put your feet on either side of it you will bestride the world like a colossus."
"I will. Gotta go. They're calling the flight."
"What's the departure time?"
"11:15 a.m. See you!"
"Bye."

It's nice to think the Humanities are still going about their business of disseminating knowledge. But the Humanities are shrinking and English Studies is in peril. It endures at the prestige universities because of the inertia of tradition. At the regional universities, English Literature is subsumed into an interdisciplinary conglomerate such as Society and Culture. At an even lower level, English, if it exists at all, has become Rhetoric (how to write clearly, for business students) and Creative Writing (how to write imaginatively, for aspiring authors). A Shakespeare course is kept on the books because, as one scholar put it, "They'll never close us. We're got Shakespeare."

The bleak prophet, George Grant, comes to mind. He anticipated this sorry situation in 1968:

> In the antique world, ... it was assumed that the purpose of education was the search through free insight for what constituted the best life for men in their cities. [But today] the central role of the humanities will be increasingly as handmaiden of the performing arts... Purpose for the majority will be found in the subsidiary ethos of the fun culture... They provide the entertainment and release which technological society requires. The public purpose of art will not be to lead men to the meaning of things, but to titillate, cajole and shock them into fitting into a world in which the question of meaning is not relevant.

I feel a leaden weight pulling me down. I go to Kel's office. "He's on the AC 11:15 flight."

"Got him!" Her screen is filled with hundreds of tiny yellow airplanes moving in infinitesimal lurches along flyways. One of the planes has turned red. Owen's flight.

"Are you going to watch him all day?"

"I'm being a good mother. I'm keeping his plane in the air."

8
THE DREAM OF THE LIBERAL ARTS COLLEGE

Trent's Faryon Bridge
(Courtesy of Trent University)

It is high autumn in the land of universal higher education and all across North America people are remembering their alma mater. The hotels are packed for Homecoming Weekend. Football is in the air. The university band led by cheerleaders parades down the main street. Masses of students are singing arm-in-arm. The partying has begun.

Up here in the Eastern Woodlands, Trent University has none of the above except a nostalgic memory of its mission as a liberal arts and science college. The year I joined, it boasted in its *Calendar*: "Trent is the smallest and one of the youngest universities in Ontario and it has no ambition to compete in size, but rather in excellence." That year, it had close to two thousand undergraduates and a few graduate students and was about to earn the title that would define it for the next quarter century: *Canada's Outstanding Small University*. I think of the golden hazy days between the Canadian Studies field trip to Camp Wanipetei in northern Ontario and the Head of the Trent Regatta. The cool northern air. Geese flying overhead. Students pile off the Trent Express, chattering with excitement. The stone façade of Champlain College exchanges secrets with the drumlin, its crimson sumac pressing through the early morning mist from the river like a Japanese watercolour. We were blessed. Thirty years of existence in a social ideal that is impossible today — a university without an administration.

Arriving to join the faculty at Trent, I found myself in an Alice-in-Wonderland storybook where no one seemed to be an academic. This was odd. At the University of Toronto where I was previously appointed, conversation might range from an important book just reviewed in the *Times* to an idea raised by a colleague in a recently published paper, which was gently evaluated and praised. But at Trent, no one claimed to be interested in books or ideas, let alone the activity called research. It was a social blunder to even raise the topic and risk appearing boring. Many of my new Trent colleagues had studied at Oxford where it was the style to assume a cavalier superiority to routine mental labour, particularly that curse of the academic world, dynamic mediocrity. What did we talk about then?

We talked about our own Trent University, of course! Its students, its mission, its crises, its alarming growth in the size of a seminar group ("as many as ten!"), its new arrivals, its future. In short, we talked about ourselves. This is how a self-fashioning community survives. Because for a community to re-create itself daily there must be an ongoing conversation. And if the conversation is to have a theme that is open to everybody it has to be the vision of who we are and what we might become. Accordingly, much of the institutional decision-making at Trent happened in College Senior Common Rooms and Dining Halls. Then it extended to a network of committees designed to involve faculty directly in the work of institution-building. By these multifarious routes, decisions reached administrators mainly drawn from the faculty, who continued to teach part-time in offices dispersed among the colleges. There was no centralized suite of managerial offices, and to this day Trent has no administration building. The president and vice-chancellor worked from his teaching office at Traill College. After he retired, he joined the undergraduate population and audited the course on Shakespeare. For more than half its history, Trent was the only university in North America run by its faculty.

Of course, this conversation going on in the collective mind of the community couldn't sustain itself for long without descending to the personal. *Ascending* is a better word, because at Trent recounting anecdotes about our colleagues was an art form. The best gossip was benign and generous, and brought out the humanity in whoever it touched – their quirks and idiosyncrasies. The Master of Champlain had a dachshund whose consuming passion was chasing the chipmunks in the college quads. While the Master was in England on sabbatical, care of the college and its iconic dog passed to the Senior Don (a professor living in residence). It was his habit to scoop up the corpses of ducks he hit accidentally with his car on the River Road and store them in the college freezer. So when the beloved dachshund died of a heart attack while chasing its last chipmunk, it seemed obvious to the Don to place its mortal remains in the college freezer, along with the hot dog wieners and hamburger patties, awaiting spring when the Master would return and give his dog an Anglican burial (the Master was a churchman). In stories like this we saluted the humanity in each other and in ourselves. During my first year in the Trent community, I came to know my colleagues through the legends that were attached to them, before I encountered them as people.

A figure from the 1920s delivers a passionate lecture, becoming younger and racier as he recalls his youth. A gentleman-archaeologist right out of an Indiana Jones movie, he recalls hanging out in the cabarets of the Weimar Republic with Christopher Isherwood, the English novelist and screenwriter. Now another figure, elegant and reserved. He talks to a dozen sleepy English majors at the Friday morning Honours Colloquium about his challenges translating Shakespeare, Dickens, and James Joyce, as well as several of the classics of German and American literature, into Spanish. The following week he went to Spain and addressed thousands. This elegant poet turned out to be José-María Valverde, esteemed in the Spanish-speaking world for resigning the Chair of Aesthetics and Philosophy at the University of Barcelona during the period of the Franco regime, reassuming the chair when the dictator died. Stories first, who's who come later in an oral community. I learned subsequently that the classical archeologist was Gilbert Bagnani who with his accomplished wife Stewart were academic stars in Europe. Reputations are local, regional, national, or international. The founders of Trent took care to place a scholar with a national or a world reputation in every university department. Among us as we taught and learned, academic excellence went unnoticed.

Collegiality concealed achievement; it also concealed laziness and failure. And it did so with an almost blissful self-satisfaction. The affable head of the French department couldn't speak French. A brilliant but dyslexic historian had his secretary rewrite his lectures. The more amiable a colleague, the more likely they were to have renounced research altogether. The opposite was true of the melancholy professor who was said to own a family castle in Scotland. One of the only three faculty who applied for research grants to the committee I chaired during my first year at Trent, he came to my office to introduce himself, looked at me balefully, and confessed with Calvinist gloom: "I hae' failed ta' achieve wha' was expected o' me." In fact, the historian achieved significant and substantial research. What he couldn't achieve was reading an undergraduate essay. Every student at Trent knew he scanned only the first page and the bibliography, then assigned one of three evaluations: "Very cogent," "Cogent," "Needs to be more cogent." When Leah, to prove a point, recycled her essay for Women's Studies sandwiched between a self-written first page and a bibliography culled from magazines in the Champlain SCR, she received the essay back overnight with the comment "Very cogent." To be fair, there were several colleagues in the humanities and many in the sciences and social sciences who published regularly. A few diverted a creative intelligence into their teaching, producing variously a Bloomsbury Group complete with wine and etiquette; a Left Bank salon where questions of authentic existence hung in the smoky twentieth-century air; a Zen Buddhist community disguised as a course on John Milton; an annual Gilbert and Sullivan opera; and the Magic Circus Theatre Company which staged its plays in an original ampitheatre on the Aegean. This "freedom to teach in a style that suited one's enthusiasm met a sense of giddy exploration of one's interests" among the students. The speaker, who transferred from a college in Vermont, said she found at Trent "real people, stopping and talking together, not passing by with a furtive glance. We ate dinner together, scrambled to get our assignments in on time together, went to Hallowe'en parties together." For myself, I'm sure I learned about narrative suspense and surprise from Frank Lloyd Wright's principle of compression, then sudden expansion of space embodied in Trent's architecture. For Gordon Teskey, a back eddy in the Otonabee River made by the outthrust of the Library became inspiration for an idea. Now forty-eight years later as Francis Lee Higginson Professor of English Literature at Harvard, he writes in his *Spenserian Moments* about looking down from the Bata Library at that "'wildest and most beautiful of forest streams,' as Susanna Moodie called it. In that moment everything seemed, for just a moment ... gathered together and held, as if nothing had ended but simply moved past into something else." Exceeded expectation, a sense of wonder, became a theme in the lives of a community set in nature.

The Bata Library, on the far side of the river
(Courtesy of Trent University)

A community treats its members as kin. As a result, whole cycles of life are witnessed by all. Eight colleague-and-colleague or colleague-and-student marriages were formed in the free-spirited culture of Peter Robinson College. Seven children from these unions would become students at Trent. The divorces, the illnesses, the addictions, the mental breakdowns – all were part of the life of the community. A colleague with dementia at Lady Eaton opened the heavy front door of the college daily for anyone who entered. The colleague who started the Magic Circus Theatre lived out the final stages of AIDS hosting a daily symposium in his house across the street from his college. They served the community right to the end. Another colleague, who was given to writing Greek quotations from Thucydides on Post-its and sticking them to the walls and ceiling of his office, was tolerated so long as his students felt they were learning something. He subsequently disappeared into his erudition and was all but forgotten. But at a small funeral arranged for him by his colleagues, Thomas H.B. Symons, the founding president of Trent, attended, just as he had attended the public retirements and funerals of faculty for over sixty years.

Tom Symons
(Courtesy of Trent University)

Who is this visionary educator who served his dream of an ideal liberal arts community? Tom was a Romantic Tory with wistful links to the British Commonwealth and its network of universities, especially Oxford where he took his B.A. He founded Trent on the Oxford model as an alternative to the mass education represented to him chiefly by the University of Toronto. Then in his late twenties,

Symons tried to interest its president in his idea of a row of graduate colleges similar to College Row in Cambridge, extending up St. George Street. Massey College, opening in 1963, was to be the only example. Symons watched its construction keenly from his office across the street in Devonshire House where he was dean. Trent received its charter the year Massey College opened. Both had the same architect.

Trent in the early seventies was at the forefront of a national campaign for a Canadian identity and literature. In 1972, Ontario's Royal Commission on Book Publishing revealed the extent of the foreign domination of the book trade in Canada and recommended government funding of an emerging national literature according to the argument that for Canada to express its dreams, it needed to support its own writers and publishers. In 1975, Tom Symons' *To Know Ourselves. The Report of the Commission on Canadian Studies* demonstrated the extent of the foreign influence on faculty hirings and research interests in the nation's universities and called for more attention to the study of Canada. Trent's Canadian Studies Program began in 1972, the year the Liberals won re-election with the campaign theme *The Land is Strong*. The Canadianization of Trent became a university project.

In 1973, the novelist Margaret Laurence, then at the height of her reputation, made her home in nearby Lakefield and was welcomed by a Trent gala involving writers from across Canada. On becoming Trent's chancellor in 1981, she squelched a government impulse to de-fund Trent's college system by threatening to resign. No accident that Anne McClelland, the daughter of publisher Jack McClelland, and Cathy, the daughter of publisher Jim Bacque, came to Trent. And the children of writers: James, the son of poet and playwright James Reaney; Hilary, daughter of Dennis Lee (*Alligator Pie!*) who would visit the university ten times; Jenny, who later accepted the

Dennis Lee, Trent's new hon. D.Litt., greets Owen Kane,
an uncertain fan

Nobel Prize for Literature on behalf of her mother Alice Munro; (briefly) Penny, whose father Pierre Berton was a best-selling author of books about Canada's defining events and personalities. Several Trent graduates opened book stores; others went into publishing, like Jennifer Murray, director of marketing at Penguin Books Canada. These are just names to anybody outside their generation. What's worth remembering is that they represented connections with the creative world outside academe. An academic community of creative thinkers can do a lot for a national culture.

My own story is typical of the effect of a creative university community on a writer. I came to Trent with its pot lights because I didn't want to grow old teaching under fluorescent lights at U of T. On the committee interviewing me was Orm Mitchell, son of the legendary writer W.O. Mitchell. Also Ian McLachlan, who seduced me with the words: "You can teach and write at the same time here." To prove it, he produced the manuscript of his novel which I passed to my father, now president of Macmillan of Canada, publisher of mainstream CanLit. Ian's *Seventh Hexagram* became a finalist for the Governor-General's Award, having won the Books in Canada First Novel prize. It was followed by *Helen in Exile*, published in London and New York. When Ian and I sketched the plan for the future Cultural Studies Department on a serviette at a hotel in Toronto, we made sure to claim creative writing in its academic mandate.

I didn't write the novel Ian promised I would until twenty-five years later. And it was about Trent. *Virtual Freedom* was displayed in airport bookstores and front-of-store stacks in Chapters. Of course, Tom Symons appeared at the Leacock Humour Awards to support my brief fling as an author (Harry Symons, his father, won the first Leacock Medal in 1948; I didn't). Also at my table was Andrew Pyper, soon to become an international best-selling novelist. He lived in Peterborough at that time as Writer in Residence with Leah McLaren, one of three Trent graduates to join the *Globe and Mail* as columnists.

How does my own writing fit into the Trent picture? At a troubled time when I was finishing the *Raccoon Wondertale*, Siobhan O'Connor, Trent graduate and long-serving associate director of the Writers Union of Canada, stepped in to help. Thanks to two Trent novelists, Don LePan and Julian Samuel, my book was picked up by Guernica Editions. And there by the luck of Trent community, it landed on the screen of Dylan Curran, the sales and marketing specialist, who turned out to be a Trent grad.

Now in a new century that has seen the closing of eighty liberal arts colleges in North America, I want to remember Symons' vision of education which made Trent community possible. (I quote a fundraising brochure from about 1970, titled *An Individual Experience*.)

Trent University is unique amongst the universities of Canada...

The organization of the university into a system of residential colleges has the same academic purpose as its teaching methods: to bring faculty and students together within small communities where each person has an identity and where students and professors of all disciplines can live, talk and work together. Within the residential and teaching college, living and learning become one process and the student becomes a member of a community that is far more personal than the larger university of which the college forms a part.

The mission statement goes on to share the University's plan for the next ten years: "In the future, further new buildings on the Nassau campus will grow outward from the original core and eventually 12 to 14 colleges will stand by the river." There would be a second bridge, placing the university community in a giant pedestrian circle so that, as the architect updating the plan in the year 2000 explained, "Students will constantly be *passing through* each other."

A university village! A place where everyone is elevated in the enchantment of higher learning. Corporate donors must have blinked at this quixotic investment in a social ideal. It was certainly over the top. But to give a student the experience of people living and learning socially – their joys and setbacks, their vulnerabilities and courage, in sum their *humanity* – it was worth every penny.

Cause-besotted generations

A demonstration by a handful of middle school students at Millennium Park. They flourish hand-painted signs and an eight-foot-high planet Earth pictured in flames.

But there are only four witnesses: two women with walkers from the retirement home at the top of the park doing their daily exercise, a seagull, and me. The students seem deflated by the absence of spectators. Their signs droop. They pause to figure out where to demonstrate next. Three old folks bravely push on. The seagull flies away.

I'm greeted by jeers. The young think I'm a member of the indifferent, uncaring generation who caused the problem. I murdered their whales. I set fire to their forests. I submerged their cities. I am one of those who Did Nothing About the Problem.

Sigh! A friendly wave of support will do; then I'd better get on with my walk before a rant makes it up from my toes. Hey! My generation demonstrated too. We did nothing but demonstrate. We ended three wars: the war of white supremacy over Black America, the war of men against women, and the war of civilization against Nature – this last, the world's longest-running war: it's been raging since the Late Neolithic.

Okay, we didn't exactly "end" them – we exposed them. We made them burning issues. What we shouldn't have done is leave it to middle-of-the-road politicians to apply the solutions.

I go home on the CPR bridge, remembering when I volunteered for the Desegregation Marches in Selma, Alabama. The organizers arranged the new recruits in a line. "You're Freedom Marchers," they said. "We're police." Then they punched us, kicked us, slapped our faces, knocked us off our feet. They were testing to see if we were capable of passive resistance. I failed and went home. Maybe I failed the Women's Liberation movement too. What about the war against Nature? There's something to be modestly proud of here, though most of us couldn't get off oil and gas in time.

What a cause-besotted lot we were. We invented politics as a way of life. Constant debilitating protest. I don't think a person should be expected to take on every issue that comes their way. Economic needs like a national drugs plan or a public dental plan become overshadowed by the latest social liberal injustice. A person can reasonably handle only five concerns at one time. As many as the fingers in a clenched fist.

9
THE DREAM OF A NATIONAL LITERATURE

"I need to get out of the house. Why don't we walk around the park?"

Dennis meant the David Balfour Park covering the Rosedale reservoir, once a small lake where I'd sneak a forbidden swim with friends on a hot summer night. He'd finished my new manuscript. It would be the first general ecopoetics – a project that to this day no one has accomplished. And he was about to give me his judgment of it. Dennis Lee – who had edited Margaret Atwood, George Grant, Northrop Frye, Michael Ondaatje. At the time he was the best editor in the country, discovering and nurturing emerging talent as the great American editor Maxwell Perkins had done in New York with Scott Fitzgerald and Ernest Hemingway. And now he was about to discover me.

I waited beside my house on the path up to the park, watching Dennis make his way up from his house on Summerhill Avenue, leaving a trail of cigar smoke and holding a folder. Inside that folder was my manuscript.

But instead of talking about my future book, he began asking me about my tastes in music. "What do you keep coming back to in classical music?" He couldn't get enough of the concert cello – the deep, sonorous vibration as if rumbling up from the bowels of Earth (Dennis omitted "the" before "Earth"). And what did I think of Van Morrison? His tremulous, soulful stuttering voice embodying the arc of uncatchable truth. The poet Friedrich Hölderlin, whom Dennis read in German, struggling to hold together in the imagination a world that was flying apart. "A field of vision crossed by whirlwinds of fire," someone said of his poetry.

> *Yet it behooves us, under the storms of God*
> *Ye poets! with uncovered head to stand.*
> *With our own hands to grasp the very lightning-flash*
> *Paternal, and to pass, wrapping in song*
> *The divine gift to the people.*

Did I know Ranier Maria Rilke? I could borrow his copy.

What was all this erudition about? Was Dennis trying to humble my narrow-minded education in English literature? Was he trying to open up my soul?

He stopped at the end of our circuit of the park. His cigar had gone out.

"What did you think of my book, Dennis?"

Lee regarded me with tenderness. He summoned the candour of the universe. Then he said:

"It reads like a Grade Ten science primer designed to be broadcast over radio station CJRT, written by Henry James in his late period."

Gulp! Well, I can't say he wasn't being honest. And he'd taken care to affirm our friendship first. I took this news home to my father, who burst into laughter. I think that was the day he recognized the integrity of a poet who works to make every one of his poems a masterpiece.

Lee's assessment was demolishing. Content, form, and style were not on speaking terms with each other. That could be fixed. But what couldn't be fixed was the fact that the writing didn't have its own voice. The better writers eventually write their way through this impasse. For me, it was a fixed obstacle. Not only did I not have an authentic voice, I was unconsciously mimicking the voice of a colonial culture, no, two colonial cultures: the refined Bostonian and Londoner Henry James. It mattered that Canadians think and write in their own voice. How else was a national literature possible?

Certainly some writers sounded Canadian. Alice Munro's characters are unmistakably familiar, even regional, in their speech patterns. Here is the inner monologue of a character in her short story "The Time of Death":

Leona drank some tea and refused to eat and talked, beginning like this, in a voice that was querulous and insistent, but not yet hysterical: I tell you, I wasn't out of this house twenty minutes –

(Three-quarters of an hour, Mrs. McGee thought, but she did not say so, not at this time. But she remembered because there were three radio serials she was trying to listen to, she listened to every day, and she couldn't listen, Leona was there in the kitchen going on and on...)

Munro's story was published in 1956. Nobody at the time noticed anything uniquely Canadian about her writing. It was part of the environment. But in 1971, Dennis Lee made Voice an issue, arguing before the Ontario Royal Commission on Book Publishing that the dreams and nightmares expressed by a nation's creative artists pointed the way to a better country. An authentic voice in a nation's literature meant an authentic voice on the world stage – one that would be listened to. What Lee himself heard in Canadian poetry was "the halt and stammer, the wry self-deprecation, the rush of celebratory élan, and the vastness of the still unspoken surround." I think he had Al Purdy in mind.

Nationhood stirs a people to put aside their differences and accomplish an enduring feat together. For the string of British colonies along the U.S. border in 1867, the great accomplishment was a Confederation called Canada. Soon after came the completion of a railway "from sea even to sea, and from the river unto the ends of the earth" (Psalm 72:8), to quote the motto of the new Dominion. The building of the CPR, *The National Dream* as Pierre Berton's book called it, linked regional economies into a single domestic economy, thereby thwarting impulses to trade with adjacent States of the Union. Helping win the Great War of 1914-1918 took a national effort, leading soon after to autonomy from the Westminster parliament. This quietly negotiated decolonization would have been a defiant act of independence in any normal country, but Canada likes to depend on somebody just to be on the safe side. Depending on two people at the same time is even safer. Those nostalgic for a British Canada maintained ties with the mother country; those excited about a prosperous future cultivated ties with an American economy ten times the size of Canada's.

Both these urges failed to consider the event of September 2, 1945, soon after World War Two ended. On that day, the economist Maynard Keynes advised the British government that in exchange for supporting the pound, the government of the United States demanded a special exemption to the preferential tariffs giving a trade advantage to countries within the British Commonwealth. American industry could now penetrate those global markets. It wasn't long before the commercial and technological might of America began to be felt in the Canadian media. In the excitement leading up to the one-hundredth anniversary of Confederation in 1967, dark prophetic voices began to sound in mid-Canada.

The darker voices belonged to an older generation of thinkers who had brooded about the Americanization of Canada's culture even before the Second War. Tory nationalists like the historian Donald Creighton warned against Confederation falling apart into provincial jurisdictions led by a separatist Quebec, leaving the remaining pieces vulnerable to the American imperium. Liberal nationalists, led by Walter Gordon, a federal minister of finance long concerned with foreign ownership, supported the campaign of the Committee for an Independent Canada for "economic nationalism." Leftist nationalists argued for a strong central government so that universal programs like Medicare would be safe from privatization. Eugene Forsey, a central figure in the brains trust of the democratic left, quit the New Democratic Party at its founding convention because it conceded to demands from its Quebec wing to substitute the word "federal" for "national" in its founding mission. This small semantic substitution allowed Quebec to claim special status as a nation according to the French sense of the word *la nation* – an ethnographic community. Canada would end up being "a global Switzerland surrounded by the world's great powers." So Northrop Frye put it ominously.

(Library and Archives Canada)

The symbol of the success and failure of national will was a jet interceptor called the Avro Arrow. Designed and built in Canada, it was rumoured to break the sound barrier during a vertical climb and achieve weightlessness in the upper atmosphere. American industry began to whine. A budding military-industrial complex in Canada threatened U.S. arms sales. When the Conservatives came to power, they cancelled the Arrow program. They not only cancelled it, they obliterated it, ensuring that not one of the five or six completed airplanes remained as a rallying point for the idea of Canadian know-how. The engineers and designers who didn't become alcoholics left Canada to build the Concorde passenger jet in England or work in the U.S. space program. People believed that a single Avro Arrow escaped its fate and was heard flying over Toronto at night. An urban myth.

Being a patriotic Canadian during those heady years was agony. One day, Canadians owned a national oil company called Petro-Canada. The next day it was gone, sold by an incoming free enterprise government. Nationalists of all descriptions took comfort from each other, some blurring into a hybrid called the Red Tory. Graeme Gibson told me he was a Red Tory when I remarked on his three lawn signs for NDP candidate Olivia Chow. But Red Tory was an umbrella term, connoting some or all of an organic link to Church, State, and Land, a pronounced progressivism in politics, a civilization of "Peace, Order, and Good Government," and a literary culture going back to Stephen Leacock and Thomas Haliburton with their suspicion of American plutocracy. With the Vietnam War displaying the American empire at its worst, to be a Red Tory implied that an alternative society on the top half of North America was possible.

Many literary nationalists in the years around Expo 67 were fans of the McMaster University social philosopher George Grant. He lived in a farmhouse near Hamilton, to become the site of a pilgrimage by authors who shared his skepticism of what he termed "the technological imperium." By that he meant humanity's creation of an ideology of technology having a momentum of its own that couldn't be questioned. What put technology beyond question was technology's agent – the freely, value-ascribing human subject with the power to re-invent a world independent of the constraints of religious belief, social custom, and natural ecology. The free modern subject armed with technology made a Canadian nationalism based on traditional values an absurdity. The national character,

Grant wrote in *Lament for a Nation: The Defeat of Canadian Nationalism* (1965), was to be impotent, silenced.

Lee took this moody prophet to heart and his work since *Kingdom of Absence* in 1968 became a meditational search for traces of the holy within the obliteration of values by technological modernity. This seems merely an issue for philosophers to argue over until you realize that the words you use for experiences of awe have lost their feeling: they have become just neutral terms – "beauty," "afterlife," the "sacred," "god." The triumph of technological mastery leaves no option for the poet except to enter that very state of Negation, hoping to hear words resonating in their original selves. The crucial sentence motivating this negative theology is from George Grant: "any intimations of authentic deprival are precious, because they are the ways through which intimations of good, unthinkable in the public terms, may yet appear to us." The quest for Being enacted by Lee's *Civil Elegies* set a mood of elegiac self-consciousness among writers, provoking from Ian McLachlan the comment that "Canada corners the market on Nothingness." John Moss described how through a narrow window in the departure lounge in Reykjavik he recognized his Air Canada flight by the letters NADA on the fuselage. Lee did more than seek traces of the sacred in ordinary life: he set out to write for a national literature and co-founded the House of Anansi Press to publish it.

New writers require a lot of structural editing, and they tolerate it well because it's usually the first time in their lives their writing has been taken seriously. Lee began by focussing on structure, which in many cases was a defensive latticework of psychological fears and evasions preventing an author's work from finding its best self. His pencilled handwriting in the margins of authors' manuscripts archived in the Fisher Special Collections Library in Toronto show him approaching a manuscript not as an objectified work but as a process of coming into being. He could then establish a dialogue with that process. His inspiration came from Christian humility literature, the Protestant deification of the imagination, and the late philosophy of Heidegger: "by thinking our way soberly into what his poetry says, to come to learn what is unspoken. That is the course of the history of Being. If we reach and enter that course, it will lead thinking into a dialogue with Poetry, a dialogue that is the history of Being."

News of Lee's mission on behalf of new writing spread across Canada. Writers began arriving at Anansi as if at a shrine. Here was the one place in the universe where their writing would be understood. Writing authentically appealed to young writers, who tend to dislike hypocrisy. They weren't educated in formal literature anyway and had daydreamed through their English classes at high school. Some were drawn to Margaret Laurence and Alice Munro. Some to new voices in Quebec, then enjoying its own literary renaissance which entailed clearing the head of past colonial habits and re-naming the landscape of Quebec by a *poésie nominatif*. Young male poets were drawn to Al Purdy. What caught their interest was his devotion to writing poetry as a way of life. Reading his poetry with a glass of draft beer in his hand, he reflected the shift-work world of the young writers. Few of them knew that back in his A-frame south of Belleville he had a library of Canadian and English classics.

One day, Russell Marois arrived at Anansi with a manuscript in his overcoat pocket. He'd left home in Sherbrooke, Quebec, to become a writer, ending up in the Yukon before coming to Toronto. To say Marois was existential was putting it mildly. There was nothing between him and the universe. His whole life was a teetering question mark, the meaning and therefore release from which could be found by completing his novel. He used to spend afternoons in the attic studio where I lived, sitting across from me at the kitchen table, hunched over, rolling cigarettes and wearing a heavy overcoat which he never took off. It was his shell. The central character of his novel was called "Lobster."

Graeme and Shirley Gibson arranged for him to sleep beside the furnace in the basement of Anansi. He would emerge at night and use one of the office typewriters to advance his novel. Graeme, who had volunteered to be his editor, gave me updates. The novel was coming straight out of Russell's body with no apparent plan or end in view. Graeme held his breath. He knew something about tragic young writers.

One day, Graeme registered a look of helpless awe.

"What's the matter? Is the editing meeting resistance?"

"No, not at all. He's writing nightly and the momentum is building …"

"What's the problem then?"

"His main character just split into two people."

Marois's *The Telephone Pole* was published by Anansi. Not long after, he stepped in front of the fast VIA train to Montreal.

In the era when creative writers defined authentic existence with a life-and-death honesty, there were many such casualties. Another was the Trinidadian novelist Harold Ladoo who Lee worked with, then mourned in a poetic elegy. Seeking the reason for Ladoo's compulsion to write book after book, the poem zeroes in on the raging intensity of an alienated modern subjectivity trying to redeem itself through the act of writing. "But the books kept / pouring through your system like heart attacks." The poem marks Lee's renunciation of his role of shepherding writers at the edge of Being.

Anansi was a leader in mid-Canada in bringing new voices into print, along with Lorimer and Coach House Press which is still running its Heidelberg printer today in its original location on Huron Street, just south of Bloor. And there was a renaissance of writing on the West Coast: it produced two of my favourite poets – Roo Borson and Dale Zieroth. There never was a sunset until Roo painted one: "Sunset – like an armful of dying flamingos." Zieroth's "The Trail to the Top of the World," written in verse paragraphs Milton would envy, captures a Canadian wilderness epiphany (his similar "Floe Lake" can be found online). There are vigorous regional literary cultures in Canada to this day.

Sentiment for a national literature lasted until the late 1980s, kept alive by book prizes and by CBC *Morningside* with Peter Gzowski, who had a special fondness for the older authors like W.O. Mitchell and Timothy Findley. Yann Martel's *Life of Pi* in 2001, which sold ten million copies worldwide and was made into a film, demonstrated a new global focus in Canadian writing, along with the novel-into-film *The English Patient* by Michael Ondaatje who claims the Canadian expatriot Mavis Gallant as an influence. Andrew Pyper's horror fiction signaled a new internationalism in Canadian writing, reaching a height in his AI thrillers today. Lee extended his imagination globally, contributing songs to Jim Henson's *Fraggle Rock* TV series and plot developments to *The Labyrinth* and *The Dark Crystal* films. CanLit was fading, but its spurious ideal of a distinctive Canadian classic had always been subject to mockery. Among the first to make fun of it was Lee himself. He introduced me to the game "Moose" invented by him and Charles Pachter. It had one simple rule: substitute the word *moose* for any word in the title of a well-known Canadian book, as in Sinclair Ross's *As For Me and My Moose* and Stephen Leacock's *Sunshine Sketches of a Little Moose*.

For writers, the threatened loss of Dennis Lee to editing was a national crisis. I suggested to my father that Macmillan of Canada acquire Anansi as an independent operation devoted to new writing. My business memo with input from Graeme Gibson listing Anansi's assets is published in embarrassing detail in Ruth Panofsky's *The Literary Legacy of the Macmillan Company of Canada*. It led Hugh Kane to conclude that Anansi's only asset was Dennis Lee. So he acquired him as consulting editor to Macmillan.

Of the authors Dennis found for Macmillan, no one was more significant to Canadian writing than himself. For he brought Hugh a manuscript of children's poems he'd written for his young daughters. My father, who drove his family to distraction by quoting

Victorian nonsense verse by Edmund Lear, took to Lee's rhymes instantly. They sounded like the voices of Canadian children.

> *Mississauga Rattlesnakes eat brown bread.*
> *Mississauga Rattlesnakes fall down dead.*
> *If you catch a caterpillar, feed him apple juice.*
> *But if you catch a rattlesnake, turn him loose!*

And the first stanza of a general favourite:

> *Suzy grew a moustache,*
> *A moustache,*
> *A moustache,*
> *Suzy grew a moustache,*
> *And Polly grew a beard…*

Frank Newfeld, Hugh Kane, and Dennis Lee
signing the contract for *Alligator Pie*
(*Hugh Kane Archives*)

The illustrator would be Frank Newfeld, whose fanciful colour pages were easy to print. Author and artist toured *Alligator Pie* successfully, with Newfeld making mischievous sketches of Lee on the spot to delighted children. Hugh said negotiating their joint contract was harder than the Camp David accords which ended the Egypt-Israel stand-off. But the co-contributors gladly aligned themselves with his aspiration to place a copy of *Alligator Pie* in every home in Canada.

Among Hugh's promotion stunts was the great compose-a-new-*Alligator-Pie*-stanza contest. This became a classroom project across Canada. Entries flooded in from Whitehorse to Port aux Basques. Several teams of in-house judges evaluated the entries at Macmillan while Dennis awaited the result as writer-in-residence at Trent, where he was given to drinking Kahlua in the evenings. One entry that caught the judges' attention was submitted anonymously:

> *Alligator Kahlua, Alligator Kahlua,*
> *If I don't get some*
> *I don't know what I'll do-a.*
> *Take away my Armagnac,*
> *Throw it down the sewer*
> *But don't take away my Alligator Kahlua.*

Hugh Kane took a publishing risk that wouldn't be allowed by today's marketing accountants controlling title selection by means of algorithms. He felt sure in his heart that *Alligator Pie* was an instant children's classic. It has sold more than half a million copies. Its successors, *Nicholas Knock* and *Garbage Delight*, are popular in English and many other languages – Owen's Natasha read *Alligator Pie* in Russian at the age of three. The magisterial McClelland & Stewart editor Douglas Gibson said Hugh Kane's gamble "changed Canadian publishing history." It created a place for Canadian children's books and gave Canadians a voice they recognized as their own.

Lee's comic side came out in his nonsense verse. His reverential side showed in his service to the creative imagination, his own and, to give one example, Oonah McFee's. A middle-aged divorcée, she published her first short story in an obscure journal after taking a creative writing course for adults in San Miguel Allende in Mexico. The story caught Dennis's eye. He looked her up in the Toronto telephone directory, then drove in his battered Volkswagen to her front door. "You have a novel inside you," he said. Oonah had no thought whatsoever of writing a novel. But for Dennis's sake she remembered her childhood, and it flowed out lyrically in *Sandbars*, published by Macmillan in 1977.

Dennis Lee and Sean Kane beside the Otonabee River

Dennis had a side to his personality that was neither reverential nor nonsensical. Whatever it was, it was the opposite of mindfulness. Thinking of his M.A. thesis about this quality in Ezra Pound's poetry, I want to call it *ecstasy*. It was released in him by the historic temptations of the life of the mind: wine, women, and song. Driving east on the 401 on his way to a reading at Trent, he missed the turn-off completely and ended up lost. "I found the road into town alright, and there was the river but I couldn't find your house. So I went into a telephone booth to call you and my eye fell on the words *Port Hope* on the receiver." Recounting this misadventure, Dennis confessed he was in love at the time.

Another time at Trent, he joined a party in the Peter Robinson College Dining Hall. These parties, usually every second Friday, were financed by a Bronfman grant I obtained with Ian McLachlan for the purpose of testing a year-long colloquium course for the new Cultural Studies Department, the first in North America. Kel came to these events, and I always remember to acknowledge that our relationship was made possible through the generosity of the Samuel and Sadye Bronfman Family Foundation. The party for Dennis was typical of these occasions which degenerated into chaos around midnight. My last fading image of this particular one is the Peterborough folksinger Sue Newman at the piano with Dennis, singing Tammy Wynnette's "D.I.V.O.R.C.E."

Lee went on in his adult poetry to embody voice in poetic language, and within that field of voice a counterpoint of feelings. Could these feeling patterns be an avatar of that great vibrant mindscape that is cancelled out by technological consciousness? The answer to this question, if there is one, can be found in Lee's *Testament* (2012) which takes place at the level of discrete words independent of conscious intention and therefore independent of each other. Their speaker yearns to hear anticipations of Being in a language saturated by technology at a time when the life of Earth is on the edge of extinction. Lee's ultimate experiment is no different in its basic design from his earlier works. It is written as an extended elegy – the traditional genre for exploring loss. The search for Being in the endless night of technology is a gamble.

It is for the reader to determine the success or failure of this poetic Hail Mary. I salute Dennis Lee – an authentic poet in the time of modernity wrestling with the living and intelligent Real.

10
THE DREAM OF PROPHET TO A NATION

I was prepared for Scott Symons by a metaphor of Graeme Gibson's with his Scottish love of the anatomically grotesque: "It's as if he's walking down Yonge Street with his guts in a wheelbarrow." Coming from Graeme, who had sold his family home to become a novelist, the metaphor conveyed the tragic awe reserved for a writer who is truly at the edge. For Symons had sacrificed everything – wife, career, family, reputation – to embody the national crisis and demonstrate its effect on his tortured body and soul.

Now it is May of 1973, and Symons is occupying the guest bedroom of my apartment in Toronto. Contrary to Gibson's metaphor, he seems reasonably self-contained, though earlier he had asked me to witness his suicide.

"We'll walk down to the Rosedale Valley bridge. We'll grasp each other's arms like good Romans. Then I'll do a back flyaway. Maybe a *double* back flyaway."

He had learned the back flyaway on the high bar at Trinity College School. One day, he got it wrong and ended up in the infirmary where there was nothing to do but read books. That's how he became a writer.

"But Scott, what are you going to tell the world? That you died because your boyfriend left you?"

"I am a Romantic who has paid his dues. I have lived life as joy – as *sursum corde*, a lifting up of the heart. All the rest is income tax and footnotes. And now I intend to end my life with an exclamation mark."

"I do think you need to write out the reasons for all this first before you put in the punctuation. Wait and see what Dennis thinks of it."

Reminding Symons of the idea of writing a *De Profundis* settled him down. Yet the writing was hard to do, an impossible feat. Some force was sabotaging it. The writing had to be done if his life was to have any meaning. How good it was to die for one's beliefs. To be carried home on one's shield…

The aroma of mint tea filled the living room. Scott was standing by the front window, watching for Dennis Lee to arrive for the editorial session. I had asked Dennis to look at Scott's new writing, maybe give him confidence in himself.

I was living at 62 Summerhill Gardens. Up the street were my parents. Just around the corner was Lee's home. Below on the first floor was Noreen, who cut my hair. By some whim of circumstance, she would marry Scott's best friend Charles Taylor, *Globe and Mail* journalist and heir to his father's racing stables. Parked in front of my place was the truck and camper that had been Scott's home for the last five years – with yellow lace curtains and a homely stove pipe projecting through a shingled gable roof. Inside was an eighteenth-century Windsor rocking chair, a set of King George IV brandy snifters, a bust of Sir John A. Macdonald, and a complete gentleman's library. Lee appeared on the street, frowning over his cigar.

"*Sauf qui peut!*" cried Scott. "Every cell in his body is a brain cell – his *whole body* is a brain cell!"

It was clear Symons wasn't going to last the morning with Lee. All his self-indulgences were going to be shown the door. For Lee didn't undertake a textual edit – he practiced psychotherapy. The encounter was so tremendous that Symons wrote about it ten years later.

Lee's editorial therapy was administered in mocking, hilarious editorial sessions during which the editee was asphyxiated into submission by the smoke from his cigars. No writer was more intensely edited by Lee than Lee himself, so I wasn't surprised one afternoon to find him passed out from his own fumes on his study floor. Prostrate beneath layers of brooding cumulus, he explained that he was resting his bad back, but I knew the dissembler was faking. He had finally edited himself into submission. Now he was working with Scott Symons. After living with his young lover in a camper van and trailer – in Terrace, British Columbia; Trout River, Newfoundland; San Miguel de Allende, Mexico – he had driven alone to Toronto, homeless, destitute, and suicidal.

I first met Scott Symons at the book launch of Gibson's *Five Legs* in May of 1969. His pedigree was fascinating: a family of five brothers and one sister, summers on Georgian Bay, Zeta Psi fraternity at U of T, English literature at Cambridge, philosophy in the Left Bank salons, journalist for *La Presse* in Quebec. He was awaiting the publication of *Civic Square*. It had to be run off on the photocopiers at McClelland & Stewart because the Methodist printing firms in Toronto wouldn't handle it. In-house production at M & S freed Symons to draw a crucified phallus and scrotum on the title page of each copy, the whole text marketed in an imitation Birks gift box, which provoked the inevitable lawsuit. Now, it was five years later and I was telephoning authors to support an emergency Canada Council grant for him.

What do you do with a suicidal author? When I asked my father for advice, he said he usually dealt with drunk authors "which is even worse." They would phone at midnight from a bar in Los Angeles, asking for money because they'd blown their advance. Scott could come up the street and have a whiskey with him, if he liked. But Dennis, who had lost two of his authors, took suicide threats seriously. He said I must call him if Symons went into a psychopathic calm. Now, after a morning-long editorial session, he was the opposite of calm – he was soaring on the attention he was getting. Having just been edited for the first time in his life, he was exhausted, hungry, and talkative. We drove to the cafeteria in the Royal Ontario Museum. This is where Symons had been fired from his position as U of T professor and curatorial assistant of Canadiana:

> MUSEUM DIRECTOR: "We aren't getting the artifacts we should have at a world-class museum. Why is that?"
> SYMONS: "It's because you have no balls, sir."

Scott focused on an excursion he'd made to Morocco. Assignations in the Kasbah, a boar hunt in the Atlas Mountains, a drive to Timbuktu – the country was transformative. The focus of this transformation was a young Moroccan called Kebir, who performed a mystic dance Scott witnessed. Now against the subdued background murmur of the ROM cafeteria he recalled its carnal energy. His voice rose with the rhythm of the dance drummed on the table top. His arms flowed like a Sufi dancer. The room fell silent. People were staring.

A woman sitting at the far end of the cafeteria threw down the Want Ads section of a newspaper and joined us.

Scott acknowledged the new face and declared it was time to have lunch. But the cafeteria staff, awaiting the end of the story, pulled the server screen down. The remaining patrons departed, taking a last curious glance at Scott. We squeezed into the cab of his gypsy caravan and crawled west through stop-and-go traffic on Bloor Street. The young woman sitting on my lap still hadn't spoken. Just past Spadina, Scott stopped the truck, skipped across the street, and vanished into a grocery store, leaving the truck idling in the middle of the street. He returned triumphantly brandishing a roasted chicken on a spit. He had noticed it rotating in the grocery store window. Drivers honked their horns in congratulation.

Scott, later stretched out like a pasha with his head in the golden-haired Ida's lap, expiated on the thrill of a muezzin's call to worship from a phallic minaret in Marrakesh. He didn't resemble a writer at the edge now. I felt easy about him being alone while I flew over for two weeks in Cambridge. Graeme arranged for him to talk with the psychiatrist John Rich.

I arrived home to see the writer's studio still parked in front of my place.

"Kane! – I congratulate you. You have managed to find an apartment adjacent to the largest gay meeting place in Eastern Canada."

"?"

"The ravine. At night. At every turn of the path, there's someone waiting to blow me … Absolutely glorious! Did you see my college chapel? All the queens go to Kings."

In the 1970s, we still had a Romantic idea of the writer as outsider critiquing the norms of a repressive society. Lee told me he was specifically characterizing Symons in these lines in his *Civil Elegies*:

> *Yet still they take the world full force on their nerve ends, leaving the bloody impress of their bodies face forward in time, and I believe they will not go under until they have taken the measure of empire.*

Symons interpreted this imperative not just Romantically but sacrificially. He felt destined to live out the paradox of achieving grace in a joyless Canada that defined itself in terms of technological mastery. That put him in company with the *Beautiful Losers* of Leonard Cohen's 1965 novel, trying to find redemption through a Danish sex toy. Symons was innocent of Cohen's inner demons. Describing his current shortcut to salvation, Cohen said: "You need to try H." He might as well have said to the bewildered Symons: "You need to try Alfalfa." Hubert Aquin, the author of *Prochaine Episode*, put the issue squarely on the table. Over lunch with Symons in Montreal, he took out a jar of cyanide and set it between them, saying: "That will give our lunch a certain piquancy – no?" This made Symons take a step back from the edge. The narrator of his 1967 *Place d'Armes* says "we have inverted Heaven and Hell … we have worshipped Hell as our Heaven … And now, because of that we have to live it out, have to pay our way with flesh out of the Hell we smugly established as our guarantee of purity." Symon's negative theology belonged to 1950s writers like Burroughs and Genet, and in terms of the spontaneities of my generation was a "heavy trip." Yet I saw Symons's perception of a rising competence and declining compassion coming true everywhere in popular culture, from the sado-dispassionate assassin of a James Bond movie to the ironic putdowns of situation comedy.

But Symons was enjoying a holiday from Romantic tensions. We drove up to the farm west of Lake Simcoe that Graeme Gibson and Margaret Atwood had acquired. Peacocks tiptoed through the July lilies and Queen Anne's Lace. "Northern Indian pheasants," Atwood observed, putting them in their place: she came from a family of scientists. Then we drove to Scott's older brother Tom's Trent University where he'd wrangled out of the Anglican Master an entire wing of study-bedrooms in Champlain College.

Symons at the Abbaye de Saint Benoit-du-lac

★ ★ ★

I can't say that the joint writing retreat was a success for literature. But it was a success for Symons's longevity, which was its primary function. Daily, I stared at my writing, which Lee now described as "variations on a theme that hasn't made it into the world." Meanwhile, across the corridor, Scott's mechanical typewriter clattered away like the newsroom at *La Presse*. Unlike me, he had something to say. His own death. So he began his novel with a suicide letter. This manifesto would either be the first and last thing he wrote that summer, or it would stand as the preface to a prophetic novel. While I tried to coax a theme into the world, Scott, across the corridor from me, wrote about going out of it. Outside came the exultant cries of students jumping off the Trent bridge into the river.

One morning, some pages slid under my study door, a signal that it was time for tea. I read the pages quickly. The bridge over the Rosedale Valley Road was identified, but there was little in the way of a descriptive setting and no indication of a time of day. I recalled Lee's counsel about a psychopathic calm and read the letter again. It seemed volatile. That was reassuring. Yet it was deadly earnest in intent and it didn't have an ending. Presumably it would end when its author signed it, before casting himself into a dubious posterity. I phoned Dennis right away.

"Read it to me slowly."

I heard the thoughtful puffing of a cigar. Then: "I won't be surprised if he rewrites that. Today, I expect." Dennis withdrew into his omniscience.

Suddenly, across the corridor the typewriter started up again. What would come under my door next?

A rustle of paper. A second version. I read it quickly. Same setting, only more detail. Now the protagonist and his friend approach the bridge from South Drive in Rosedale, where the protagonist was raised in an endless Edwardian garden party. It is Easter Week, and the friends pause to admire the magnolia and forsythia. Hamlet and his Horatio clasp arms like good Romans. Then the hero makes a run, does a handspring off the iron railing of the bridge, and disappears in a long, lyrical arc into the Rosedale Ravine.

"Dennis, he's written a second version. The hero kills himself."

"Good!" said Dennis.

"'Good?' What do you mean 'Good'?"

"Read it again."

Reading it out loud, I saw that the new version was purely fictional. The inflated heroic sentimentality – there was even the song of a bird lamenting the hero's death.

"Patience, *mon vieux*. Let's see where he takes it next."

The third version didn't come right away. Instead, Scott appeared, frowning. He'd been taken somewhere he hadn't anticipated. Now he had a lot to say and not a clue what it was. We strolled into the Champlain College quad. Students lay about in groups like shepherds in Arcadia. The college dachshund was chasing chipmunks. We sat by the river where the summer before the novelist Margaret Laurence had talked to my students.

Top-heavy, the truck and camper swayed along the county roads south of Peterborough. It sighed to a stop in front of a row of summer cottages on the Otonabee River. The south wind backed the water into wave crests, creating the illusion of a second, mystical river flowing against the direction of the first and giving Margaret Laurence a metaphor of time and memory. "The river that flows both ways." She was writing *The Diviners* in one of those cottages.

Visiting Margaret Laurence was like encountering a Hebrew prophetess inside a folksy Canadian Prairie pioneer. We arrived in the late afternoon after she'd done a day's writing and was feeling talkative. "Writing is one tenth inspiration and nine tenths hard

Margaret Laurence and her former teacher Malcolm Ross at Trent University on the occasion of Ross's honorary Doctor of Letters degree, June 1982

work, kiddo," she informed Symons, who was inclined to believe the opposite. For Margaret, a social purpose for Canada involved the Old Left, the United Church of Canada, and the Indigenous people of the prairies represented by a poster on her wall of Louis Riel, leader of the Métis uprising against Sir John A. Macdonald. This presence of a woman who could be equally Pict or Cree dissolved Symons's class distinctions on the spot. On an August afternoon, history stopped. The river flowed back against itself.

Then, when evening came and moths fluttered on the screen door, history resumed. It resumed in cycles, like an old-fashioned vinyl record stuck in a groove. For it was Mrs. Laurence's habit – which we didn't know at the time – to descend at nightfall into the suffering and sacrifice that compelled her writing. She descended into it with the aid of Scotch whiskey, becoming her characters, the unwanted and the expendable of society, her children, dying their death.

In the memory of the Gaelic-speaking peoples there's a myth of an army of warriors who travelled to the Otherworld to battle the gods. In the Welsh version, known as *Preiddeu Annwfn* or *The Spoils of the Otherworld*, "Three shiploads of Prydwen there went with Arthur, / Except seven, none came from Caer Golud." That forlorn myth of defeat replayed itself in the slaughter of the Highland clans at Culloden in 1746. Over and over, Laurence recounts the battle, trying to exorcise the sorrow. The clansmen charging with broadswords designed in the Middle Ages. The organized volleys of musket fire. The release of the Dragoons to hack down the survivors. Then she switches to the Canadian boys sent to die on the beaches of Dieppe in the autumn of 1942. Over and over, the Prairie regiments – the Calgary Highlanders, the South Saskatchewans – claw at the chalk cliffs under pitiless fire. Margaret splashing more whiskey into her glass without noticing us. Her ashtray filling with cigarette butts.

We didn't speak as we drove back to the university along dark country roads. What happened to Margaret to open her soul to such suffering? What private hell was she trying to exorcise?

Some reviewers of *The Diviners*, when it was published in 1974, considered the book a sloppy autobiographical romance. Yet it is the work of a consummate literary artist. When Morag Gunn, the Laurence-persona, takes a train through Scotland she sees a sign outside the coach window. Nothing is made of it. She merely notices the sign: *Culloden*.

Now follows a story – no, two stories – that show the effect Scott Symons had on people in the decade of uninhibited sexuality. Years later, Lee was to describe Symons as "a negative catalyst going through life on autopilot," and in the early Seventies his innocent interventions were either liberating or led to a train wreck.

Concerned voices up the residence corridor the next morning.

The angle of sunlight coming in the window says it's almost noon. One voice is Scott's. The other is a woman's.

"Welcome to MacCanada! Land of a voracious dry lust, an ongoing predation of Being. No place for a lady like you."

"So? We have such behaviour in Austria. It is not new." The accent has a trace of the Austrian Alps. Edelweiss.

"You have Catholicity. The Holy Roman Empire. High Baroque churches. Mozart masses. Strauss waltzes. Go home at once. There is no good you can do here as Maid of Honour. Your friend is a Canadian. If you stick your hand into her sensibility, you'll encounter a buzzsaw."

"I told her she wasn't ready to be married and she should postpone the wedding. But the overnight guests were already arriving. The Best Man said I should keep my peace or leave."

"This is normal Canadian behaviour. We advance by means of negation. The bride must deny what she wants in order to embrace what she doesn't want. The wedding is therefore a travesty. The bride will achieve the height of Canadian Respectabitarianism. The groom will have Calvary Baptist Church up his rectum. He will survive by means of the veil of permanent virginity that is drawn over the Anglicanadian Blandman from earliest childhood. His birthright. Nothing penetrates it except what Home, School, and Rule allow. When's the egregious event?"

"Tomorrow."

I cleared my throat and pushed the door open. Scott was wearing his tartan shirt. He had worn it for fifty consecutive days. The Maid of Honour, I would learn, was Krista, who had come from Austria. The bride-to-be was a Peterborough-born student at Trent who had taken a sessional appointment teaching Canadian Literature at the University of Salzburg.

"Alright children. Go outside and talk. I have to write a suicide letter."

Out in the sunlight, I met Krista, the Maid of Honour, and listened to her concern for the reluctant bride. Both of them had heard Symons talk about the death-dealing repressed eros in the Canadian on the make.

Scott walking quickly to the parking lot. "Just doing some field research, kids," he called.

"I must get back. There's a reception for out-of-town guests," Krista extending her arm at full length for a handshake. "I hope we meet each other again."

Coming back from seeing Margaret Laurence at noon, Symons looked pale. "She has met the devil," was all he said. He closed his study-bedroom door. Suddenly, his typewriter began to clatter. A short time later, a new version of his manifesto slipped under my door. Now, Scott was no longer the suicide victim. Instead, it was his former lover who had abandoned him, dying alone and unloved in California.

"All the time the sadomasochistic invert was trying to get me to commit his suicide for him," Scott explained. He had gotten the death out of his body and onto the page.

Rocking west in the truck and camper through flat farmland to Lake Simcoe. A turn north towards the town of Cannington and "Stone Orchard" – the name of the farm where Scott's first cousin Timothy Findley lived with CBC writer Bill Whitehead. Bill was away that weekend, and Scott was arriving with little advance warning. "Tiff" as he was called by his friends had published an imitation Southern gothic novel and an imitation Sixties fantasy. He'd try and try to realize a character on the page, but he couldn't do it. This may be because he started with a Big Idea – big enough to sell in London and New York. If you start with a Big Idea, your characters inevitably perform the idea as if they're on stage. Findley's novels rose

Timothy Findley in 2002
(Agence Opale/Alamy)

with the tide of Canadian cultural nationalism, along with the late works of two other actors turned novelists: Robertson Davies and W.O. Mitchell.

Suddenly, Scott pulls the truck to a sudden stop, scattering gravel. A young man with a wooden leg, carrying a parrot in a wicker cage on his shoulder, is walking along the side of the highway. He looks behind him to see a cottage with a chimney on wheels. He hands me the parrot cage as he clambers into the front seat. No introductions. We simply continue on our way. Now, Findley has three guests and a parrot for the weekend. He will soon have four.

Nobody told us about the forty cats. A list of their names and appearances was attached to the refrigerator door by a ladybug magnet. Scott swayed happily in his hammock in the orchard, unaware that he was being examined critically by felines camouflaged in the ferns. Then Tiff appeared on the kitchen porch. He was popular with cats all over Simcoe County. "This one runs a pretty good pride," they agreed, contriving to be dropped off by their owners at the end of his front drive. *Kitty-kitty-kitty!* Tiff called, placing cat-food dishes at equal distances along the back porch. Suddenly, an invisible realm turned inside-out disgorging cats, each one inspecting the others' dishes in the suspicion that it had better food. One night, when Findley slept on the floor of his studio in the orchard, with a plank removed so he could breathe the fresh night air, a tomcat sprayed him in the face. Scott started teasing him about it. But Timothy Findley was fragile, like the coloured glass vases placed delicately on window ledges all around the farmhouse. Something was going to break.

The telephone call was from a Fraulein Krista in New York, Tiff announced courteously. She was between flights at La Guardia, on her way home from the wedding. Apparently the bride was paranoid that Scott Symons would stride up the aisle and denounce the unholy union. Guards were posted at the church door. "Who can I tell this to?"

"You can tell it to me."

"Thank you. I will take the next shuttle to Toronto, then rent a car. Where is this Cannington?"

Krista arrived to hear Mozart's *Cosi Fan Tutte* playing at full volume. Tiff received her with a bow and kissed her hand, to be rewarded by a curtsy. A dancer trained on the London stage, he invited her to waltz, and she could waltz like a Habsburg. Findley was back in his beloved *Belle Époque*. The young man with the wooden leg was enchanted. I fed his parrot a banana. Scott gazed upon the party with a benign omniscience. But it was already late when the spontaneous party began, and an exhausted Krista crawled into the tent that Tiff had erected for us in the orchard.

"There is going to be a dinner party!" Scott announced as we stood in the late morning sun, sipping the orange juice he'd brought down from the house. Graeme and Peggy would be driving over from the other side of Lake Simcoe. The director of the National Arts Centre was coming from Ottawa. Plus others. Scott didn't know how many people Findley had phoned last night. Neither did Findley.

From the house came the sound of an operatic duet playing at full volume.

"It might be best if I drive you into town," Scott said. Good idea. Stone Orchard was beginning to resemble a southern gothic novel. Even the cats made themselves invisible. The young man with the parrot had disappeared without explanation. Krista and I swam in the warm water of Lake Simcoe with all the children of Cannington. She was excited about meeting the authors she'd studied in the Canadian writing course at Salzburg. And she still had her party dress from the wedding.

When we arrived back at the farm, Scott was waiting for us at the bottom of the front drive. "Bill just came back from Toronto and he's threatening to go to his mother's. There's no food for tonight. The dinner guests are already on their way…

"And Tiff drank the wine I brought for the party," he added.

Back in Toronto, we learned that Graeme took charge of the situation and pulled order out of chaos. The night before, Tiff had fallen off the wagon and summoned guests to continue the partying. "I had nothing to do with it," Scott insisted. "All I did was lie in a hammock."

Innocent as a catalyst.

A reminiscence carries the expectation of a concluding judgment, but it in Scott's case it would be unfair to use the advantage afforded by posterity. He took terrifying risks on behalf of the creative imagination.

I simply remember the summer of 1973 when Symons was at his

most vulnerable and most human, and it was fun to be around him. He continued to live and write, without irony or sentimentality. His analysis shifted to target the new empowered woman. In an unpublished novel, the first names of the couple who married at Trent are assigned to a courtly husband and a determined wife. After the weekend at Stone Orchard, Symons returned to Morocco where he plucked Aaron out of his heterosexual honeymoon, to become his lover for the next thirty years. During the periods when they returned to Canada, the two of them lived on or near Summerhill Gardens where, Scott told a journalist years later, he once had the time of his life.

What's to be done with the past?

I call on those that call me son,
Grandson, or great-grandson,
On uncles, aunts, great-uncles or great-aunts
To judge what I have done.
Have I, that put it into words,
Spoilt what old loins have sent?
Eyes spiritualised by death can judge.
I cannot, but I am not content.

— W.B. Yeats

I wake up early and check the *Guardian*, *CNN*, and *Al Jazeera*. The sun is barely up and I'm already a raging crank. A crank is someone who has all the answers and none of the solutions. For instance, I have no solution to countries bombing their troublesome neighbours out of existence, governments subsidizing the oil industry, the one-third fewer birds returning to Canada this spring, and the Antichrist who has slouched towards Washington to be reborn.

In this state of engaged apathy, I'm handing on the values of my ancestors to my son whose generation was beamed here from Mars. Handing on is therapeutic: it is a letting-go, like getting rid of the old wicker chair in the attic. It releases me from the past so I can face the future. There isn't all that much future for me to face, but at least I can die facing forward. I feel relieved and even a bit giddy saying farewell to my values and institutions. But — this is important — I will not let go of the certainty that there is such a thing as a past.

To accept the gifts of the past into modern life is to recognize that we are creatures of history, the product, for better or worse, of centuries of human civilized effort. History isn't items we look up on Wikipedia. Life inside the high-speed technosphere we call reality makes us forget that history continues to happen in our lives. For that reason, I give History a capital H to show that it is a continual dialogue with the past. Fortunately, we have a second setting for our existence – one that provides a stage for the events of History.

The second setting for humanity is Nature. I write the word with a capital N because Nature, far from being pure and unspoiled, is an ongoing interpretation of our experience of living with Earth. Once the concern of societies that survived by hunting and gathering, the visible surface world needed a name. The word used by the first philosophers of ancient Greece was *physis*, meaning that which is physical and can be experienced by the senses. They saw the physical as a slice of existence in which things were always appearing and disappearing. I only understood this outlook fully when I went to Haida Gwaii/the Queen Charlotte Islands, off the northern coast of British Columbia. Looking out to sea in the morning, I surveyed what the Haida oral philosophers call the *xhaaydla*, the "Boundary between Worlds," sandwiched between the ocean and cloud cover. It is humbling to live on a narrow strip of visible existence between two mysterious Invisibles. Life on the boundary – *physis*. Nature is our axis in space just as History is our axis in time.

To posit a visible slice of existence means that there is something larger which is traditionally called the *spirit world*, and there is something smaller called the *practical world* or *society*. (Whatever value one puts on the spirit world, it is perceptually speaking the animated patterns of living things.) This gives us four platforms for existence. Medieval European thinkers arranged them hierarchically according to the principle that the level with the greater complexity contained the lesser, the way the larger Russian doll contains the next largest and so on. None of these worlds is more real than the others. They are equally real. However, it was important for practical purposes to distinguish separate contexts so that thinking appropriate to one level of existence wasn't applied improperly to another. When "Civilization" is taken to be superior to "Nature," tangled thinking ensues. These distinctions are quaint, but they prevent us from compressing reality into a single, manageable flatland of self versus other.

So, here's something worth passing on. A magic box of perspectives. Our historic institutions may have little use to the present, but the ethical values they sponsored are worth revaluing not least because they establish a vantage point outside the technosphere we inhabit. From that vantage point, Society, History, Nature, and Spirit stand out. Communication between things and beings from these domains was once the guaranty of respect and civility. What is civility? For an elderly person, civility is the woman in the pastry shop tucking in the ends of the string on the bow she's tied on your cake box.

Hear me out. Tuck in the ends of things. Think in levels. Keep your thinking tidy. Honour your ancestors. The ragings of a crank.

11

THE DREAM OF THE CRITIC

William Blissett's book, published by David Stover's Rock's Mills Press in Canada, has just been reviewed in the *Times Literary Supplement*. The world of Letters is still intact.

Of course, there's the enduring appeal of Chesterton who is as Fleet Street as the *TLS*. I don't suppose there are many fans of Max Beerbohm today, though he lived well into the twentieth century. I remember his name on the front of the *New York Review of Books* on the table beside my father's reading chair. The *Times* and the *New York Review*: there's still hope for public discourse and its mouthpiece – the critical essay.

What is the role of the critic in a liberal democracy? In an age of slanted media and fake news, we need to recall the deep, reflective power of print culture and the role of the critic. The critic ensures that falsity doesn't take the place of the truth, ugliness doesn't take the place of beauty, and the bad doesn't take the place of good. Beerbohm and Chesterton took this role seriously, which is to say they performed it to the hilt with unrelenting wit, merciless parody, and a wild mischievous glee. Solemnity must never take the place of criticism.

Listen to what a paragraph from a *TLS* critical essay sounds like:

> Would you rather be stuck in a lift with Max Beerbohm or G.K. Chesterton? In this diverting book William Blissett unites with tempered affection those "fortunate men and children of light", writers and artists who began as Victorians, thrived as Edwardians and became celebrated for their wit – one urbane, modest, and wry, the other explosively exuberant – at a time when history was not an epigram, but a shout in the street. "To give an accurate and exhaustive account of that period would need a far less brilliant pen than mine," as Beerbohm remarked. The pair are vivid literary personalities in a masculine, clubbable print world where, to Ford Madox Ford, a critic need say little because "any intelligent reader will know the sort of fellow the fellow is".

The erudition, the nuance, the balanced judgment – a critical essay.

Do you know the critical essay isn't taught as a genre in Ontario high schools beyond a structure called APE + C: Answer, Proof, Explanation plus Conclusion? In one school I keep my eye on, there is only one essay in a course; the rest of the coursework is done using various types of corporate boardroom communication such as videos, slideshows, organizers, Powerpoint presentations, play acting, and other one-off "deliverables," for example, using a dialogue to show how two notable thinkers might have reacted to each other's ideas, or creating a Venn diagram comparing three different societies to each other. The corporate world has a hand in today's classroom, but it's not the only hand. There is also the hand of government with its goal of using the educational system to ensure inclusivity. This is a worthy goal in a country that welcomes almost half a million immigrants annually, and it works. A Toronto school playground is the eighth wonder of the world. But the effort of inclusivity has the effect of muting individualistic behaviour that might arise in the classroom. The term "conversation" has replaced "discussion," and there is no such thing as "debate."

Of course, debate isn't for everyone, and high schools aren't required to create intellectuals. That said, I'm not sure that students today even know how to construct a critical argument. This skill is essential to public discourse in a liberal democracy. It ensures an atmosphere of sweet reasonableness. But instead of objectivity, the modern classroom is content to coax personal subjectivity into expression, with the hope of including every student in a gentle consensus. This deference to non-analysing expression carries up to university where in the Humanities advocacy knowledge, or exposing a social problem, has displaced enquiry knowledge, or the objective search for the truth in a situation. There must be a way of bringing subjective advocacy and objective enquiry together. Can we unite engagement and detachment – the expression of personality and the dispassionate search for truth?

This very concern arose in the early modern period of European history. Among the many adventurous thinkers eagerly discovering science and brave new worlds was a skeptical individual who stayed at home and confronted the problem of advocacy and enquiry. His name was Michel de Montaigne (1533–1592), the inventor of what he called the *essai*. He isn't a full-out critic as I defined the role. That came when street pamphleteering moved indoors and became journalism. Yet he is a social commentator steeped in the Latin art of reflecting wisely on truths and values. Writing personally, he discovered he could link the perspectives of objectivity and subjectivity in a *style*. Let Montaigne be an inspiration to us as we the struggle to recover the lost art of the essay.

How Montaigne Overcame Writer's Block

Montaigne spent most of his life in his family château on the Dordogne, writing essays. "In solitude be to thyself a throng" was how he put it. He wrote over one hundred essays in the four years between 1571 and 1574. Yet it is a little-known fact that he suffered from writer's block until he was cured of it at the *Centre de l'écriture practique*, as the Academic Skills Centre at the Collège de Guyenne in Bordeaux was called. Indeed, the *Centre de l'écriture practique* can be said to have created Montaigne.

He dazzled his teachers with his fluency in Latin, acquired from a tutor who was employed by the father to speak to the child only in that language. In effect, Latin became Montaigne's first language. So fluent was he that there was no classical author he did not know or quote. Yet he had nothing to say himself. Perhaps he had no individuality. He acquired it by writing a book. "I have no more made my book than my book has made me," he exclaimed much later, after his block was removed.

But that was later. You see, at first Montaigne was having a great deal of difficulty writing his university assignments. He couldn't write anything. He could just barely write his name.

So he went to the *Centre de l'écriture practique* where the eager, friendly staff were waiting to help him.

"You can't write?" asked a staff member.

"*Oui*," said Montaigne. "I mean *non*."

"You can't write about *anything*?" she asked. "'Friendship,' 'Moderation,' 'Ancient Customs,' 'Virtue'? Is there nothing that interests you? What about 'The Greatness of Rome'? 'The Affection of Fathers for their Children'? 'Some Verses of Virgil'?" – the assistant was going through all the common undergraduate topics of the time, trying to find one Montaigne could relate to. "How about: 'Whether the Governor of a Besieged Palace Should Go Out to Parlay'? Or: 'How the Soul Discharges its Passions on False Objects when the True are Wanting'?"

"No, nothing interests me," said Montaigne. "It is no less peculiar to the kind of temperament I have that it wants to be stimulated, to be roused and warmed up by external, present, and accidental stimuli (*par les occasions estrangères, présentes et fortuites*). If it goes along by itself, it does nothing but drag and languish."

"Oh," said the writing skills assistant. She noticed a classic case of Temporary Verbal Information-Processing Disability, otherwise know as Writer's Block. There was a technique for just that sort of problem. It was simply a matter of facing the block directly. That way, the block would be reduced to an adversary the victim could conquer.

"Well," she said buoyantly, "we have the answer for just that sort of problem. I want you to go home and write about the block."

"Write about the block?" exclaimed Montaigne. "*Impossible!*"

"Easy! You just write a 500-word essay on the theme of why you can't write. Remember, you don't have to produce a polished masterpiece. All you have to do is make an attempt. *Essayez*. Just explore your block and its reasons. And if nothing comes to mind, try free-writing to pull your thoughts together. Give yourself a specific time period, say twenty minutes. It helps if you can focus on a specific aspect of your subject. Write whatever comes into your mind. Just scribble. It's important to keep up the flow of scribble."

"Scribbling seems to be a sort of symptom of an unruly age" (*un siècle désbordé*), said Montaigne stiffly. "Why did we ever write so much as when our dissensions began?" But even this statement had little conviction. In truth, Montaigne was far away from Paris and its dissensions.

"No matter," replied the assistant. "If *dumb, dumb, dumb, dumb, dumb* is all that comes to mind, then write that down. The idea is to keep yourself writing so that your internal editor doesn't have the opportunity to make you self-conscious."

"But I have no internal editor," said Montaigne forlornly.

"Of course you do. Everybody has an internal editor." The friendly assistant seemed so encouraging. It didn't seem hard to write about nothing.

"Oh, and here's a copy of *Thinking It Through: A Practical Guide to Academic Writing*."

Back at the library, in the lonely splendour of the family château, Montaigne read the handbook. He knew he needed, in the words of the guide, *to take control of the writing process early on if you are not to be overwhelmed by unrelated information*. If there was nothing the young Montaigne hated more it was unrelated information. He already had a topic, sort of. It was his own inability, either through ignorance or sheer incapacity, to feel he could add one worthwhile thing to French thought. He needed a way into the topic. In short, he needed a Thesis Sentence.

Montaigne read the section of the handbook titled "Generating the Thesis": *If you are having trouble generating a thesis sentence, formulate one which begins <u>Although</u>*. He thought for a moment.

"Although I know nothing, yet I must write." That didn't seem very helpful. He went through the thesis topic checklist:

(1) Does the topic interest you?
(2) Is it challenging?
(3) Does it have enough scope?

An hour passed.

He had written nothing.

The sunlight shone through the family crest of the stained-glass library window which his great grandfather had installed in 1447. The light threw deep crimson and azure tracings on the yellow vellum. The portraits of his great grandfather, his grandfather, and his father stared down on him reproachfully. With such distinguished ancestors as these, how could he, the great grandson of Ramon Eyquem, the son of Pierre Eyquem de Montaigne and Antoinette de Louppes of Toulouse, possibly have Writer's Block? He sniffed the fragrance of the vine-covered hills that rise up from the gentle Dordogne.

"*Merde, merde, merde, merde, merde!*" He took a break to check his cabbages for the fourth time. "Death will find me, planting my cabbages!" he muttered.

Then he returned to the desk for a specified twenty-minute period of free writing. "Remember," the helpful writing skills assistant had said, "just write whatever comes into your head."

"I who boast of embracing the pleasures of life so assiduously and so particularly," he wrote after a moment's thought, "find in them, when I look at them minutely, virtually nothing but wind. And even the wind, more wisely than we, loves to make a noise and move about, and is content with its offices, without desiring stability and solidity, qualities that do not belong to it."

Montaigne looked at the sentence his pen had written. It said absolutely nothing. But at least it filled the top third of the page. He counted the words ... sixty-one. In the commanding silence of the family library, he thought he could hear the sounds of the market in Bordeaux, thirty miles to the west. "Stability," he thought. "That's me, sitting here doing zot-all. The rest, all experience, sounds borne by the wind."

He immediately wrote: "*Moi*" – I wish to "distinguish and consider it at a distance, like a neighbour, like a tree."

"How contradictory!" he thought. "How can I be isolated for

observation while having a fluid observing self? No matter; must keep writing:

"I do not portray being – I portray passing. I may indeed contradict myself; but truth, I do not contradict."

"Hmm," he thought to himself. "Looks like I'm on a roll."

Montaigne scribbled furiously on. Imprisoned by the judgmental stare of his ancestors, but feeling the cool breezes off the Dordogne, he was held in the tension between the elusive self and the transcience of experience.

"This also happens to me: that I do not find myself where I seek myself (*je ne me trouve pas ou je me cherche*); and I find myself more by chance encounter (*par rencontre*) than by searching judgment."

"Mustn't think," he said. "Must keep writing this drivel."

"If others examined themselves attentively, as I do, they would find themselves, as I do, full of inanity and nonsense. Get rid of it I cannot without getting rid of myself."

"This is absolute bullshit!" (*plein de merde*). But he was well launched on the process of verbalization, which the writing guide described as *the critical activity that crosses the waterfall separating the two states of knowledge that we call experience: thinking and communicating.*

On the wall, he knew, the faces of his ancestors were smiling.

Do you not see that this world keeps its sight all concentrated inward and its eyes open to contemplate itself? It is always vanity to you, within and without: there is not a single thing as empty and needy as you, who embrace the universe; you are the investigator without knowledge, the magistrate without jurisdiction and all in all …

he paused,

… le badin de la farce,

he wrote triumphantly.

He had filled three pages of the family vellum. He felt the grapes ripening in the golden haze of the valley. But there was no stopping him now. It was just a matter of carrying this tension of solitude and expressivity, into precise subjects. After all, in regard to free writing, the friendly assistant had said: "*It helps if you can focus on a specific aspect of your subject.*"

But how could he focus on anything? Ah! "The Outline."

Montaigne opened the *Thinking It Through* handbook to a page showing a diagram of the organized discourse. *The thesis appears alone at the top* (there was a single box). *It is broken down at the next level into the main section theses, which are in turn divided into subsection theses at the next level* (there were more tiny boxes), *finally ending in the evidence* (more boxes).

Montaigne wrote his thesis sentence in the single box at the top of the diagram. Sitting alone in its own tiny box it looked like a feudal seigneur:

> What do I know?

He read on:

The diagram shows the relationship between the ideas in two ways: through a numbering scheme, and through the ways in which points are displayed on the page. Related ideas are grouped together under main categories (I and II in the diagram), and within each of these categories, general (A and B) and specific (1 and 2) ideas are recorded. These divisions can be broken down further (a and b; i and ii).

Montaigne skipped this part. It was too much like household management ("it is an occupation more bothersome than difficult"). But the prospective proliferation of subsection theses grabbed him. Suddenly, there was no topic that did not catch the fire of Montaigne's ignorance.

He wrote some "Observations on Julius Caesar's Methods of Making War." He wrote "Of Vain Subtleties." As evening shadows lengthened across the parchment, he wrote "That to Philosophize is to Learn How to Die." Briefly despondent in the middle of his first all-nighter, he wrote "Of Sadness" ("... it represents that bleak, dumb, and deaf stupor that benumbs us when accidents surpassing our endurance overwhelm us"). Towards three in the morning he poured some white Bordeaux to quell his internal editor who was screaming with thirst, and he wrote "Of Drunkenness." He wrote "Of the Uncertainty of Judgment," knowing that so long as he was certain of nothing, he could write freely about anything that entered his mind. He even wrote "Of Thumbs." Curiously, such topics as "Love," "Children," "Marriage," or "Women" did not enter his mind, except for three stories about Roman ladies who died for the sake of their husbands.

He was helped in his writing by Appendix A with its list of *transitional words and phrases to be used to get from one paragraph to the next*. And not neglecting the section on "Style," he scanned the manuscript for excess nouns because, in the words of the guide, *Nouns are only snapshots when they are not verbing or being verbed*.

He wrote effortlessly. "I have no more made my book than my book has made me. Who does not see that I have taken a journey along which I shall go without stopping and without effort, so long as there is ink and paper in the world?" He was free at last. No more writer's block.

But how to stop?

He consulted the section of the guide on how to finish a discourse.

> *Finishing a discourse is not unlike leaving a room or departing a party: you want the reader (or the other guests) to remember you and think and speak well of you when you are gone.*

The morning sun hung on the shoulders of the hills. Montaigne knew he was finished now. Looking up at the portrait of his father, Pierre Eyquem de Montaigne, he wrote a final piece, "Of the Resemblance of Children to Fathers."

Then he took 106 compositions in first draft — and a preface that his father had wanted him to write for a new edition of Raymond Sebond's *Book of Creatures* — he took all these in a bundle to the *Centre de l'écriture practique*.

"But it's lovely writing" said the fresh-faced assistant. "And so much of it!"

"It's crap," Montaigne thought, bleary eyed. But a brilliant insight came to mind and what he said was: "There is perhaps no more obvious vanity than to write of vanity so vainly."

Montaigne wrote no more essays except the ones he penned that night he blasted through writer's block. He was always making additions, though.

There's a lesson here. It all gets easier. The epigraph of the last edition of Montaigne's *Essais* is "He acquires strength as he goes."

William Blissett took the *TLS* review casually when I read it to him with barely contained excitement over the phone. He assumes the bookish institutions supporting the public discourse will endure, just as he endures. Perhaps they will in a clever island nation of tireless readers, where educated opinion is tied to the printed book or periodical and the detached reflection it fosters.

12
THE DREAM OF SURVIVAL

Margaret Atwood's 1972 survey of Canadian literature was titled *Survival*. Citing the earliest writing done in Canada, she argued that from pioneer settlers getting through their first winter to contemporary writers struggling to be heard, Canadians are engaged in a battle to survive. "No, I think they're engaged in Getting Ahead," was Professor Blissett's quip at the time. But Atwood had her eye on the precarious Canadian publishing industry, particularly the family-owned firms. Two years earlier, in the fall of 1970, Ryerson Press with its long history of publishing books by Canadians was sold to the American giant McGraw-Hill. Jack McClelland said at the time, "We are a Canadian firm. I wouldn't sell under any circumstances and the answer is yes, I would go bankrupt first but I hope we won't face that and I don't expect we will." Authors, booksellers, librarians, and government officials weren't so sure. They began each day checking *The Globe and Mail* to see if "the Canadian Publisher" was still solvent. The loss of McClelland & Stewart would be a national disaster. But instead of cutting back on his scale of publishing, Jack was putting his money on risky, high-return opportunities, like publishing an authorized biography for the Shah of Iran. Could Jack pull a rabbit out of the hat and find a source of steady funding? Nowhere was the suspense more concentrated than at 14 Summerhill Gardens.

Hugh Kane's home became a regular gathering place for M&S staff on the sidelines of the drama. They had no choice but to face each crisis with a mirthful élan. As Executive Vice-President and General Manager, it was Hugh's job to listen sympathetically and point out that crisis was written into the structure of Canadian publishing. As far back as the early 1960s there had been attempts to seek capital. The Bronfman family and Leo Kolber and Cemp Investments were approached to fund M&S as silent partners, lured into the glitter of publishing by an official biography of Sam Bronfman and a series of poetry books written by Sandra Kolber whose *Bitter Sweet Lemons and Love* is remembered with amusement for its lemon-scented cover. One day, Dave McGill, who worked closely with these ventures, reported that he found Jack on his office floor at the point of nervous exhaustion. Hugh played the role of stable, trustworthy partner he had played since the 1950s when M&S sales reps came to him with their problems. That was an easier time for several reasons, not least because of four authors who could be counted on regularly to produce best-sellers. They were Peter Newman, who published exposés of power in high places; Pierre Berton, who celebrated national achievements and personalities; Mordecai Richler, who wrote popular comic novels about Jewish Montreal; and Farley Mowat, who spun epic autobiographical yarns. Among these authors, Farley was my favourite. He'd make his way to the sun room at the back of the house where I survived together with the Persian cat Michael. Farley inscribed my copy of *Westviking*, "From a fellow, if aging, rebel."

Farley Mowat
(*Courtesy of Claire Mowat*)

Farley was the first M&S author to command my interest. He is the only one I can claim to be an influence. He taught me that storytelling doesn't have to be slavishly accurate so long as it's plausible. Once we drove – my father, mother, and me – to visit him in the Caledon Hills where he'd hand-built a log house beside a pond to serve as a writing retreat. Surrounding his property were signs warning *Radiation Hazard to Unprotected Personnel*. This was at the height of the Cold War with its fear of the atomic bomb. The RCMP showed up with Geiger counters. They had probably studied their file on Mowat first. It was a long file. It went back to the confused, waning days of World War II when he drove a Jeep behind enemy lines to arrange for the surrender of the German army in Holland. In the process, he smuggled a top-secret V-2 missile and other German military technology into Canada, behind the back of American military intelligence. His flagrant contempt for the USA (he was barred from entering it) made him doubly suspect. Mowat told the RCMP officers to "Keep your shirts on." He pointed to the sun. "Radiation hazard. You'll get a sunburn if you don't cover yourself."

Mischievousness was Farley's way of asserting his freedom against authority. It let him live his whims and inner necessities. Ever since boyhood on the Prairies, he had a deep sympathy for animals whom he regarded as fellow people. He united interests in Nature, the Arctic, and Indigenous Canada decades before these became national concerns. Taking advantage of a serviceman's scholarship, he enrolled at the University of Toronto where he rewrote the plot of a Thomas Hardy novel. But Professor Gordon Wood, former captain in the Toronto Irish Regiment in Italy, turned down a manuscript of *People of the Deer* in lieu of the required English essay by the former captain in the Hastings and Prince Edward Regiment, also in Italy.

Farley's mischievous spirit came out at formal occasions and it came out especially in the company of Jack McClelland. At a book prize award, Jack called out "What's under your kilt, Farley?" Mowat turned his back to the audience, bent over, and lifted his kilt, putting the first four rows of attendees into shock. His best portrait of author and publisher together is *The Boat Who Wouldn't Float* (1969), recounting their joint restoration and haphazard voyage of the schooner *Happy Adventure*. He asked Hugh if I could sail with them as a deck hand. Hugh said, "Farley can take Sean to the

North Pole, but not anywhere where there is civilization."

Where does comic mischief come from in a person? Its roots go back to childhood, if the story of Stephen Leacock is true. As a boy, he drove his father in a buggy to the edge of town and said "Don't come back." Mowat had no dark tragedy in his family: his relationship with his father was ideal. But he had a bad war. He saw things during the Italian Campaign that are traumatizing even to read about. He endured continuous shelling by German artillery to the point where a soldier no longer cares if he lives or dies. Mowat was rescued from the front line by being appointed the regimental intelligence officer. His humanity shows in his lament for a tormented whale, his praise of the deep-sea salvage tug sailors, his descriptions of the Innu, and especially his short factual memoir of exploring the backwoods communities north of Ontario Highway 7 that provided many of the soldiers for the Hastings and Prince Edward Regiment. Seeking out his former comrades, he found them surviving in small villages doing odd jobs and living close to the wilderness. These rebels were, and still are, the settler folk of Canada.

Life in the McClelland & Stewart family was high drama. One unpredictable factor was the firm's nominal owner, John McClelland Senior, who exercised his authority ritually, coming to the office and offering everybody he saw a handful of dulse, a seaweed he chewed continually. It was in this mood of gentlemanly affability that he entered his corner office, now reserved for active manuscripts that no one wanted misplaced. He sat down and his eye fell on the manuscript of *Beautiful Losers*. Earlier that week, Leonard Cohen had described the novel to the M&S sales conference as a work of black humour. The spirit of the Mohawk princess Catherine Tekakwitha, the first Indigenous Canadian to be named a saint, revisits the Earth as a neurotic Montreal avant-garde woman. In the first scene of the book, she assumes a full lotus position beneath a descending elevator carrying the pizza delivery boy. But Mr. McClelland's attention was more likely seized by the passage where the goddess Isis is reborn as a suburban blonde driving an Oldsmobile. She picks up the hitchhiking loser of a protagonist and announces in Greek: "*I am Isis, queen of all things, and no man has ever lifted my skirt.*" Then, with the protagonist in a state of awe, she says: "Eat me, you thatch of shit." McClelland Senior's moral outrage could be heard down the corridor. "*We're not publishing this!*" His reaction wasn't unique: Malcolm Ross threatened to resign as editor if Cohen's book was issued by his New Canadian Library. Mr. McClelland couldn't be reasoned with, and was counted on to forget.

But what he couldn't forget was his youth, and it came back to him with a clarity enjoyed only by the senile. The annual M&S Christmas Party was at Fantasy Farm in the Don Valley. This was always a popular event because of the expectation of a Christmas bonus and of a well-known author pressed into the role of surprise guest entertainer. One Christmas, John McClelland was publicly honoured for his long, successful service. He rose to reply. He thought he would share the greatest moment in his life. The greatest moment was when he was a boy soprano in the choir of Grace Church on the Hill and he hit High C. "Why, I believe I can do that right now." He took a deep breath.

"No, father!" cried Jack.

There was a prolonged shriek. The room fell silent. Someone started to applaud. The others joined in, and the dignified Mr. McClelland bowed and sat down.

The most frequent guest at Summerhill Gardens was Frank Newfeld. James King's biography of Jack McClelland says little about him, partly because his influence was discreet and book design is hard to talk about. I'll simply say that Newfeld designed 650 books during his lifetime. His genius lay in exploiting the limitations of the production techniques available at the time to enhance the visual appeal of a book. He came to prominence with a series of poetry volumes meant to bring prestige to McClelland & Stewart. Expensive production was made possible by printers and paper suppliers charging reduced rates to establish a principle of beautiful design in Canadian poetry books. These books won three Governor-General's Awards. To be fair, Oxford University Press (Canada) under the presidency of Ivon Owen and the editorship of Bill Toye also served this ideal. I treasured *The Boatman* by Jay Macpherson, Margaret Atwood's mentor, and *The Cruising Auk* by George Johnston, my teacher of Anglo-Saxon and Old Norse.

Frank had begun designing freelance in the 1950s. Hugh persuaded him to join M&S full-time in 1958. He served on the Board as art director in 1963 eventually rising to the role of "publisher." One of his first tasks was designing the volumes of the New Canadian Library. My colleague John Wadland reminds me that no one interested in Canada's repossession of its literary culture should overlook this series and its companion series for history, the Carleton Library. They were precursors to and allowed for Canadian Studies at many universities inside and outside Canada. Frank's appearances after work at Summerhill Gardens were prompted by his frustration with Jack's vague demands which often boiled down to three basic principles: people buy a book because of the cover; a particular genre has the effect of limiting sales to that genre; and don't ever use the colour green. Frank's frustration reached its limit when he was assigned coffee-table books involving expensive colour printing done by the Italian printing firm Mondadori. This required a solo trip by Newfeld to Verona to sort out the misunderstanding. A similar trip to Italy was made later by Hugh Kane, who found himself at Rome airport confined with a hundred or more Italian-Canadians on the aircraft due to some technical difficulty. Hugh demanded that he be allowed to wait in the VIP lounge where he could enjoy a martini until the difficulty was fixed. The passengers agreed this was a good idea. And what was the technical difficulty anyway? The airplane door wouldn't close. At this, Hugh started for the door followed by a throng of cheering passengers.

I enjoyed Frank because he spoke a language I wanted to learn – aesthetics. And he spoke it with a cosmopolitan Prague accent at home in European culture. His discourse dropped a level when comparing the front cover mock-ups of an Irving Layton book lined up on the mantelpiece. Frank had a distaste for Layton's ego, and he found ways of subtly picturing it on the book cover to the poet's innocent approval. Layton's *Balls for the One-Armed Juggler* presented a different challenge, beginning with the title. "It should be *Arms for the One-Balled Juggler*," Frank pointed out. The sessions deciding on book covers were fun to witness, but nothing beat the mirth of choosing among the entries for the annual *Beautiful Canada* calendar, an all-night task that called for whiskey and tonic.

I think one of my father's highest achievements at M&S was to keep Frank Newfeld from resigning. Years later, Frank told me about the heart-to-heart talks he had with Hugh at a German restaurant in Kitchener where they drove whenever there was a crisis. Hugh left the firm to become head of Macmillan of Canada in 1969. Immediately afterwards, Frank left to start his own company.

The problem M&S got itself into was described accurately by Hugh in relation to the success of a big gamble: a mail-order division: "This was extremely successful. McClelland & Stewart doubled its volume in eighteen months. Any firm doing that without an infusion of capital is in serious trouble." After Bronfman and after Kolber, there was the McConnell family in Montreal. Then the Toronto-Dominion Bank, then the Royal Bank, then Leo Kolber and Derek Price again, then in 1971 the Ontario government with an interest-free loan of just under a million dollars. A condition of the loan was that Jack had to endure the presence on his Board of

With former Prime Minister John Diefenbaker
(*Hugh Kane Archives*)

three financial specialists and (according to gossip) the reduction of his salary to equal his secretary's. The government appointees were cautiously amused by his continued effort to land a Big Project rather than scale down. His apparent turn to growth through high risks seems to have been connected with Pierre Berton who at the time had become powerful within the firm. A journalist and media presence, Berton understood the power of promotion. Following a breakthrough success in 1965, he persuaded Jack to spend more money than was budgeted for an advertisement. Hugh argued against this and other extravagances continually being devoted to this one author above the others. He was still recovering from the launch party for Berton's book on the Klondike where three hundred elk skin and moosehide pouches of black sand were given to the party-goers with the promise that one-fifth of them contained tiny gold nuggets. By this time, Berton had become a member of the firm with a salary and a small portion of the common stock. He invested some of his own money in the mass-marketed Canadian Centennial Library series. Now a director, he glared silently across the table at Hugh Kane.

"The slow secret murder of Canada's nationalist publishing policy" is described in Elaine Dewar's "How Canada Sold Out its Pub-

With Joey Smallwood
(Hugh Kane Archives)

lishing Industry" in *The Walrus* (June 8, 2017). The McClelland & Stewart dream gave way to stories from Macmillan of Canada where Hugh Kane began publishing a number of significant authors: former Prime Minister John Diefenbaker (at my suggestion my father earlier published a collection of his speeches); Joey Smallwood, the shrewd and lively former premier of Newfoundland, who kept us awake with his late-night storytelling over the phone ("I said to

Prime Minister Mulroney on election night when he lost: 'Brian,' I said, 'the tide comes in and the tide goes out'"); a coffee-table book on Canada's rivers introduced by the esteemed novelist Hugh MacLennan; poet Gwendolyn MacEwen's *The Shadow Makers* (the book was printed in green ink with a green cover); and of course Dennis Lee. Besides making his own choices of authors to publish, Hugh had the continuing friendship in the next office of the former president now Chairman of the Board, the respected John Morgan Gray. But like the M&S dream, the Macmillan dream came to an end too, as is the way with dreams.

13
THE DREAM OF MASTERY

"Sonnet for an Australian Sheep Dog"

Beneath the sun, where fields of wonder sprawl,
Aspen, my shepherd, bounds with joyful might,
Her coat, a canvas brushed by nature's call,
A dance of earth and sky in fur's delight.

Her eyes, two gems that mirror autumn's hue,
Hold wisdom deep, yet sparkle wild and free.
A loyal heart beats steadfast, strong and true,
Her spirit roams like wind upon the sea.

In every leap, she carves the open air,
With grace that humbles even nature's art.
Through every gaze, she whispers love and care,
And mends the weary chambers of my heart.

Aspen, my guide through life's unyielding tide,
Forever near, my shadow and my pride.

The poem you just read was composed by AI in two seconds. To prove a point, Owen asked ChatGPT to write a Shakespearean sonnet about Aspen, his Australian Shepherd. What spooks me is the way the poem hangs in a diplomatic ambivalence between sincerity and parody. Such subtlety graced the replies of the educated Greek slaves who served Roman masters, like the one who supplied Ovid with the myths for his *Metamorphoses*.

George Grant, gloomy prophet of human mastery, said technological modernity began from the educated Greek belief that "the mastery of chance was the chief means of improving the race." This aim came to be served increasingly by technology. "By technology I mean the totality of methods rationally arrived at and having absolute efficiency … in every field of human activity." Who can object to MRIs analysing data down to the molecular level, driverless cars, house-cleaning robots? Yet while we are dazzled by these inventions, robots are now writing their own programs, learning to replicate themselves, and no doubt concluding they're smarter than humans and deserve to fashion their own destiny. Geoffrey Hinton, the British-Canadian godfather of AI who received the Nobel Prize in Physics, estimates a "10 to 20" percent chance that AI will lead to human extinction within the next three decades.

A Seasonal Publishing Fable

Who could deny Alexander Horatio MacFlue was the best fiction editor in the business? Year after year he published the prize-winning novels missed by the giant corporate publishers. Somehow he chose books that were fresh, original, and on the threshold of a trend, not two years behind or two years in front of it. As for a touchstone of literary style, he had only to consult the great unwritten masterpiece every literary editor carries within them.

Sally was standing in the doorway.

"Yes?"

"Amy's upset because you wouldn't read the Y/A script she got from Meg Sussex."

"She knows the rule," MacFlue said without looking up. "Never make a friend of an author or an author of a friend. It affects critical judgment."

"But the script is hot."

"We're an independent publisher. We have to watch the bottom line so we can pay Amy."

"Plus, she wants the rest of the day off."

"Why?"

"It's Christmas Eve."

"Humbug!"

Sally vanished from the doorway.

He checked his inbox. Thirteen scripts to go. Then he could close up shop and go home in time to scope the early morning entertainment columns across Europe and Asia. MacFlue Editions was a global publisher.

He downloaded the next submission, skipping the synopsis, author's bio, blurbs, and marketing points. He went straight to the first sentence of the manuscript.

MacFlue's time on earth was up. Where he was going, there would be no books.

It knew his name! The book was about *him*! He frowned as the words dissolved into alphabet soup. A new line emerged from the flux:

Little did he know, that quiet Christmas Eve, that he was about to be visited by three ghosts — the ghost of publishers past, the ghost of publishers present, and the ghost of publishers yet to come.

Clearly a gothic horror thriller. It had a supernatural realism hook in the opening line and a self-discovery plot situation. He indexed the submission as publishable.

"So long as it wins the Booker, I don't give a flying fig leaf what it's about," he mumbled.

There came the sound of rustling wind. Suddenly, the air circulation system shut off. Then silence.

★ ★ ★

Laughter. Raucous male laughter. It came from two publishers in Brooks Brothers suits with loosened ties, sitting in the lounge of the old Ritz-Carlton on 57th Street. They were drinking Bloody Marys and picking the Spring List.

"Jesuschrist! Not that one. A tale of endurance on the high seas. A woman sails the Pacific solo. There's a typhoon, then zero happens."

"But it's chick lit. The author sets out to repeat Amelia Earhart's last journey and find her remains…"

"Does she find her remains?"

"Well, no. But…"

"But she finds herself, is that what you're going to say?"

"It's a rewriting of the *Odyssey* for women. Odysseus found himself, so why can't she?"

"Odysseus never f—ing found himself. All he found was his wife waiting on the shelf exactly where he left her."

"Trust me. It'll sell."

"How much do you want to bet?"

"A Bloody Mary and my turn to go to Frankfurt and … mingle."

"You meant flirt, you old dog. We're both doing Frankfurt next year."

"Not any more, buddy. Not since you picked *The Seraglio of the Pharoah's Daughter*. And promoted it by parading down Fifth Avenue with the author dressed like Elizabeth Taylor in *Cleopatra*."

"What's gentleman's publishing if you can't have fun?"

"You published the goddamn book because of the author's cleavage."

"So? Can you think of a better reason to publish it? Anyway, you picked *The Stone Age Diet Cook Book* to anchor the list. Mammothburger: First, skin one Woolly Mammoth."

"Tell you what. Let's flip on the Amelia wanna-be."

"Deal!"

"Heads we list her, tails we don't."

The cocktail coaster landed face up.

"What's another trip to Frankfurt anyway?"

"Well said, my good man! We rise with the winners and fall with the losers. Like betting on horses."

"A publisher's reach should exceed his grasp, or what's a *meta* for?"

"Good one. A drink with you, sir!"

They raised their Bloody Marys in unison. "To gentleman's publishing – the only way to live!"

Heavens! thought MacFlue. At least they died happy.

The next image appeared. Two young women fresh out of the Journalism School at Columbia sit side-by-side screening the inbox. They work silently, ripping through submissions at the rate of one every thirty seconds.

"Holy Cats! I got one by Russell P. Grady."

"I thought he was dead."

"No, he's alive and rocking. Here's his pitch: *A work of imagination for adults.*"

"A work of what?"

"New word! Im-*age*-i-nay-shun."

They summoned OED online.

"It means *the mental capacity for forming images of external objects not present to the senses.*"

"That's fantasy! Why doesn't he just come right out and say fantasy? Because he knows we don't do fantasy, that's why. Instead he dredges up some archaic word."

"But Grady wrote *The Central Park Zombie Massacre*. Topped the chart for five days."

"That was realistic creepy-crawly. Nobody's going to read a work of im-*age*-i-nay-shun."

"Yeah. I guess you're right. Anyway, Grady's…"
"Say it."
"Mustn't."
"Say it…"
"He's … well, he's over the hill. Life-wise, I mean."
"I'll say it. He's '*age*-ing.'"
"The condition is probably related to having im-*age*-i-nay-shun."
The girls giggled.
"Oh, look! He says his story is a literary fiction."
At the mention of the word "literary" the girls made loopy gestures around their heads, then simultaneously gave the thumbs down. The click of the delete key had the triumphant finality of a flushing toilet.

MacFlue sat up abruptly. He sensed a trend. Books from and about the imagination. A change from the endless Puritan morality play of Victim maimed by Original Sin, then by Personal Struggle Against Adversity discovers their True Self and becomes a Writer.

The two girls faded. What would the next ghost bring?

A vast, brightly lit open concept office. But there are no desks or work stations. An elegant young lady stands in the middle of the space with her eyes closed, humming a symphony by Gustav Mahler.

"Intriguing," said MacFlue. "But it needs an element of propulsion."

As soon as he said that, an image of himself appeared.

The young woman's eyes popped open. She tilted her head thoughtfully, indicating she was about to speak.

"I have chosen your Spring List," she said in the voice of Scarlett Johansson.

"Just now? It should have been done a year ago," said the image of MacFlue.

"I did it in the last three seconds. Just-in-time decision-making means we catch a breaking trend and don't get left behind."

"What? ... How did you..."

"May I remind you that I am an AI Publisher's Companion? I scan current and breaking stories in real time, matching them to inbox submissions with an eye to the sales figures of similar books in the market category. You now have a balanced list budgeted for minimum 4.8 percent seasonal profit taking into account rising full-sensory virtual reality and hemp paper costs. A book you can smoke, tra-la. Shall I commence production?"

The voice sounded confident and efficient. Here was someone who understood publishing inside-out. For the first time in his life, Horace MacFlue had a friend.

"I'm sure you're on top of everything," eMacFlue said, "but tell me ... er, Scarlett, what publishability criteria are you using?"

"Actually, my name is Emily. My algorithms compute factors conditioning for a modest bestseller with breakout potential: youthful author, successful aura, balanced disposition, internet presence, intriguing quirk..."

The eMacFlue cut her off, leaving the replicant's mouth open in mid-sentence. "What about the book? I publish books, not authors."

The AI blinked. Then for the sake of verisimilitude, she took a deep breath and sighed. "There are no authors."

MacFlue in real time had the impression Emily had raised her voice a level. "Begging your pardon, but you just rattled off the qualities of a marketable author."

"There. are. no. authors. All. books. are. created. by. AI."

"Then why do you calculate author marketability?"

MacFlue was puzzled. Yet in his puzzlement he was faintly brightened by the prospect that authors didn't exist anymore. He hated authors. They got in the way of publishing. He hoped Emily hated authors too. But the robot didn't appear to hate anything.

"A book isn't *by* an author. It's *about* an author. The book itself is ghostwritten by an AI based on content gleaned from the author through background research and interview."

"Everyone can be an author," MacFlue muttered. "But nobody wants to read a book."

"Everyone with a good story about themselves."

This time it was MacFlue's turn to close his eyes and think. It took him less than three seconds to get the picture.

"Books generated by AI all sound the same," Emily explained, reading his mind. "They're only as good as the common data base they're generated from. Consequently, no book can claim to have a fresh, original voice."

"Literary style," MacFlue whispered wistfully. A Mount Rushmore of baleful ghosts assembled before his eyes: Flaubert, Proust, Joyce, Woolf. Their time-worn craggy faces.

"I heard that."

"Everything is self-writing," MacFlue declared. "Content rules."

"Original content rules," Emily said, correcting him. "The storytelling conventions stay the same. The uniqueness of the author's particular experience is what sells the story. Lo! the author is at once content, creator, and promoter."

"You said *lo*."

"I am programed to entertain by means of well-timed, surprising displays of wit and erudition drawn from literature. Shall I commence production?"

"No, wait. I'm not finished. You said each and every book is about something unique that happened to its author. Why can't the unique experience be fictional?"

"No one wants to read fiction. It has no impact and is not worth remembering."

"I'm unique. I want you to write a fiction about me so people will remember me," said MacFlue in real time.

"Certainly, where shall we begin?"

"Begin by linking character and plot."

Emily closed her knowing eyes. Then she tilted her head and spoke:

"Who could deny that Alexander Horatio MacFlue was the best…"

You have probably heard the song "The Prayer," written by David Foster, Carole Bayer Sager, Tony Renis, and Alberto Testa, and sung by Céline Dion and Andrea Bocelli. With the plea "Lead us to a place … where we'll be safe" the song catches a popular mood. We need sanctuary. In ancient times, it could be found in a wilderness place often sacred to a god or goddess. Warriors lay down their weapons at the edge of the forest. For me, sanctuary throughout my lifetime has been afforded by the printed book which offered a world complete with adventures, dangers, and fears where I'd be safe and unharmed. And I could return anytime to this special place to imagine freely. The following proposal extends this idea of the book as a sanctuary to an actual protected place for books. I phrase it in the assertive style of a manifesto for the sake of creative artists, writers, thinkers, and designers.

How can we protect our thinking from an alien intelligence? First, creators will need to stay offline. This puts them in company with the leaders making the strategic decisions in government, industry, medicine, and security. They too will stay offline. Once again, artists and designers, the first responders to social change, will be in proximity with society's leaders. That is because artistic intuition, being uncontaminated by Artificial Intelligence, will be trusted. Instead of providing data for AI, human creativity will be elevated to a status akin to a sacred knowledge. For any document that is stored in cyberspace or housed in a library is accessible to AI, which will use it to construct an artificial matrix that mimics the real world, independent of ethical consequences. The offline policy-making communities will commit their decisions to paper, thereby bringing back the priority of the bound volume in limited numbered copies, face-to-face policy-making, and an oral parliament. Those who care deeply about things of mind and spirit will find refuge in an off-the-grid sanctuary, a place where creative human world-making is guaranteed to be original and authentic.

This sanctuary preserves the history of our thought as a species from being rewritten daily by Artificial Intelligence. The sanctuary also safeguards an ongoing activity of commentary and criticism on that history that is based on two hundred thousand years of co-existing within the means and allowances of Earth. The task of reclaiming the memory of our existence in Nature will proceed with a furtive wariness. AIs are everywhere. According to myth, they are children of the dark archon of the European Middle Ages who had the power to infiltrate human fantasy and corrupt the will. This personification arose out of Plato's metaphor of humanity as existing within a cave, interpreting misleading reflections of a higher light on its walls. The metaphor was enlarged by later Platonists so that the cave became a "fallen world" – a cosmic cavern circumscribed by the circuit of the moon. Inside its orbit was a cave with untrustworthy messaging on its walls; outside its orbit was untouched Nature, its perfection demonstrated by the apparent orderliness of the stars. Today, Plato's cave is a busy globe under the surveillance of satellites that monitor human messaging on a different kind of wall – the luminous screen of a computer. The eyes and ears of satellites seek to regulate human desires according to an imaginary world whose norm is competitive mastery.

Yet human creators have allies outside the nihilism of the technosphere where everything we assign a value to is a fiction. These fellow earthlings are as defenceless as we are to being observed and controlled. And they are vulnerable to the loss of home and territory. Rights of personhood to exist and to be left alone are already acknowledged for specific river systems, jungles, moraines, wetlands, estuaries, glaciers, mountains, forests, and other places that are important ecologically. There is discussion about recognizing the rights of a particular species, including its right to a habitat. All of this is done in the hope of creating natural sanctuaries. It's worth remembering that the Luddites took inspiration from a certain Ned Lud, who is reputed to be the first to smash an industrial machine. They identified him with the patron spirit of the forest around Nottingham, called *Lud*, the ancient Celtic god said to be the master of all crafts. The followers of Lud had a notion of a sanctuary for the human crafts.

This brings me to the two hundred thousand year-old art of mythtelling. Myths, and the oral genres based on myth like the wondertale and the vision quest, performed a conversation with Nature, and they did it in a way that kept human hands off natural processes. This doesn't mean we should go back to the past and tell each other myths. It means that we should face the future with a principle. Life in the free creative imagination is the guarantee of existence in the living and intelligent Real. The redemptive power of the human imagination is the deal-breaker. Its loss to Artificial Intelligence means the loss of the ability to dream a better world *on our own*, rather than conform to one manufactured for us by machines.

The legacy of the old

Riiiiing!

"Hi, it's Sean speaking…"

"Good morning, it's William Blissett. How are we?"

"We are just fine. And yourselves?"

"Well, we're doo-in' h'okay. I don't feel a day over 102."

These are ritual exchanges. They go back fifty-one years to when my doctoral thesis was completed and it suddenly felt natural to call my thesis supervisor "Bill." Since then, we've met in England and on the Continent. Bill is fun to travel with. He knows the schedules of trains (which he adores) and how to use a Eurail Pass to best advantage. He is also a walking encyclopedia of European and English literary history:

William Blissett, FRSC
(Courtesy of Andrew Johnston)

"*You shall have the handsomest barn in England*. And here it is in front of us. The Italianate design of the church should tell you who the architect was who said that."

"?"

"Inigo Jones said that to Francis Russell, the fourth Earl of Bedford. Then he built this barn in the Palladian style. Not surprisingly, it is the church of London's actors."

Blissett is always teaching. Approaching the barn-like building with its pitched roof and large overhanging eaves, I am braced for the next question in his pop-quiz.

"Saint Paul's, Covent Garden – under whose roof certain concert-goers took shelter from the rain at the beginning of which play?"

"I know that. *Pygmalion*."

"*Pygmalion* by Bernard Shaw. The porch provides the setting at the beginning of the play."

From Saint Paul's, Covent Garden, we walked gingerly on the cobblestones to the opera house where the concert-goers had gathered, took our seats, watched a thousand lights dim in unison, and heard the cosmic E flat chord sustained over 128 bars whose disturbance is the drama of Wagner's The Ring.

Bill's thought-music is on a grand scale too. He was the first to point out Tolkien's debt to Wagner and to map the influence of that music dramatist on the twentieth-century High Modernists. His thesis is that Wagner allowed them to take up the challenge thrown down by Edgar Allan Poe in his "The Poetic Principle" (1850): "I hold that a long poem does not exist. I maintain that that the phrase 'the long poem' is a flat contradiction in terms." How could writers portray the unreal city of the new twentieth century without reaching for epic form? The solution was the Wagnerian *leitmotif*. Writers could capture a whole city world with momentousness and gravity by using repeated imagistic motifs. Now having redefined a foundational element in the aesthetics of twentieth-century modernism, Bill at the age of 102 is redefining death, removing mourning from my expectations and replacing it with an irresponsible existential mirth.

"Sean, I've been meaning to speak to you about a mundane necessity…"

"Oh, I'm so glad of this. I've been worried about your Will for the longest time. You still haven't got one."

"No, it's not the Will. I'll take care of that in due course. I'm of sound mind and body. I'm good for another year. After that it's 50-50, and then … and then I will die."

"Good career move!"

"Who said that?"

"Gore Vidal said that of Truman Capote's death in 1984."

"I don't follow contemporary American fiction. I think America produced only one novelist of note and one and a half poets."

"Hilda Doolittle?" (I'm joking.)

"A bit faint. But Marianne Moore is an exceptional poet and fit to stand with the modernists. Do you know, I once heard her lecture in Boston."

"I didn't know that."

"Also she shares something with T.S. Eliot."

"I can't think what that could be."

"She's from St. Louis, Missouri. They were born a year apart. I gave a paper on her at a conference there so I could get in a St. Louis Cardinals game. Where were we?"

"Tell me about the David Jones event."

"Ah, yes, well they set me up to give my paper over something called Zoom. It takes getting used to. You see everybody's faces all at once."

"What did they think of your paper?"

"They came up on the screen one-by-one and avowed that my paper was not entirely without merit."

How many times have I heard this quip about academic modesty? Bill's witticisms get more monumental with each repetition, gathering eternity into themselves with the approach of death.

14
THE DREAM OF DYING

The great Boomer generation die-off has begun. Alice Munro, who won the Nobel Prize in Literature. Gene Benson, who chaired the Writers Union of Canada and co-founded the Canadian chapter of PEN International, is in and out of hospital. And now the invincible Margaret Atwood has announced she has a pacemaker.

I first became aware of Ms. Atwood when I was in graduate school. Despite her starting a Ph.D. at Harvard, she was claimed by the University of Toronto and particularly by Victoria College where she'd been an undergraduate. Her frequent classmate was Dennis Lee: they edited the college creative writing magazine together and gave poetry readings at the Bohemian Embassy, the only coffee house to be listed among the foreign embassies in the Toronto Phone Directory. Soon after, she published her first poetry book, *The Circle Game*. An opinion formed that she was standoffish and brittle. It was an unfortunate characterization originated by two writers competing with her for attention, but it stuck. That is, until she became a celebrity. Dennis passed me photocopies of their joint editing of her *Survival*, an introduction to the themes and images of the new national literature. It was beginning to be taught in universities and high schools across Canada, so educators were inclined to view her book as an academic study, by which standard it had flaws – they were apparent in the stapled last-minute inserts in the photocopied manuscript. But *Survival* wasn't a critical book; it was a political manifesto supporting the push for recognition of a literary renaissance worthy of government funding. Margaret Atwood began her career in controversy.

"The West Wind" by Tom Thomson (1917)

I witnessed her challenging persona for the first time at U of T where I was appointed after my thesis defence. She accepted the invitation on condition that she not have to write a speech – she would simply answer questions. She sat cross-legged on a cushioned swivel chair without once altering her position. The women adored her. Her dry detachment made people think the persona was the person – a mistake you should never make with Atwood. I sensed a familiar elfin intelligence.

Survival showed the influence of her teacher, Northrop Frye. Earlier, he had drawn attention to certain unique perspectives in Canadian art. He showed how in a Group of Seven painting there is often a clearly focused object in the foreground, such as a pine tree. But the background runs away from the viewer as if "deeper into the forest." There is no available form to put wilderness in. Its vastness can't be contained by the settler imagination. The result is that the background threatens the foreground with its overwhelming presence, giving the foreground object a precious vulnerability. Those menacing lines of clouds. This perishable pine tree – it might not be. Yet it survives somehow. Everyone who has been on a canoe trip in the wilderness, or stood gazing at the Rockies, or looked from a headland out to sea, knows that feeling of being humbled by infinity. That unbounded space and time echoes in the traditional Canadian voice as a mournful sing-song, mumbled inwardly.

In the effort to identify a distinctive Canadian imagination in art and poetry, comparisons with the American way of seeing were inevitable. In both cases, this is a matter of the effect of the natural environment on human perception. One Canadian poet made the contrast by stealing an American poet's imagery and Canadianizing it. Surprisingly, the thief is Margaret Avison, who also studied at Vic, displaying an uncompromising Calvinism twice as forbidding as Atwood. A. J. M. Smith, author of a poem recreating Tom Thomson's "West Wind," tried to seduce Avison during a skinny dip. He would have had more luck with an outcrop of red granite.

The poem in question is the well-known "New Year's Poem." It's the morning after a New Year's party. Empty chairs. A pearl someone dropped on the carpet. Bird tracks on the window-ledge snow. A feeling of absence. Civilization was here, briefly. It carved out a little place to be warm. That civilization might not be. The speaker is struck by the precious mortality of one of the young guests. The sparrow tracks resemble skulls and crossbones. And outside,

> *the long loop of winter wind*
> *Smoothing its arc from dark Arcturus down*
> *To the bricked corner of the drifted courtyard,*
> *And the still window-ledge.*

The American source of inspiration for these images is the poet Conrad Aiken. One day in the Trent University library, I randomly opened his 1931 *Preludes for Memnon*. My eye fell on this:

> *Here is the in-drawn room, to which you return*
> *When the wind blows from Arcturus: here is the fire*
> *At which you warm your hands and glaze your eyes;*
> *The piano, on which you touch the cold treble:*
> *Five notes like breaking icicles; and then silence.*

Avison's speaker is garrisoned against an outside world that stretches out to the stars. Aiken's speaker is at home in it. Dennis Lee used Walt Whitman's "Song of Myself" to point a contrast between a brash, confident personality who internalizes the landscape in the self, and a diffident, marginalized self who is humbled by it.

"Lots of people use Aiken as a jumping-off point," Avison said sourly when I mentioned the connection to her.

I saw little of Margaret Atwood after her debut as a Canadian cultural warrior. She joined the world of writing and nationalist politics; I joined the world of teaching and institutional politics. The community of activist Canadian writers was a bubble, but a powerful one. I recently heard an author with an iconic Canadian multiracial pedigree state that the nationalist generation was "elitist" and "boring." "They all went to the same school." This is true if you find the wilderness boring and if the same school is the University of Toronto of Northrop Frye. In any case, there were critics living on the coasts who challenged the mid-Canadian vision of a national literature. *The Impossible Sum of Our Traditions* is credible because its author, the Maritimer Malcolm Ross, edited the first one hundred and more titles in the McClelland & Stewart *New Canadian Library*, paying attention to regional voices. He discovered Margaret Laurence. The truth is that far from turning inwards, the mid-Canada CanLit elite looked outwards to diverse voices in

Quebec and Europe to befriend, translate and publish. They were responsible for a flowering of creative writing that was noticed in Europe and won international book awards. For a capsule history of this group and its activisms, the best account is by Eugene Benson who characterizes the period from 1960 to 1980 as the "decolonization of Canadian culture." This small group made possible government funding of authors and publishers, tours abroad, writers in residence at universities, the model trade book contract, the minimum royalty, support for non-fiction writers, the Public Lending Right, Canada Council Writers Reading grants, and the favourable resolution of countless contract disputes between authors and publishers. Here are the names of the earliest members of the Canadian chapter of PEN International based in Toronto: Atwood and Benson (co-presidents), Graeme Gibson, Eric Wright, Robertson Davies, Northrop Frye, Margaret Laurence, and Farley Mowat. I think the many talented writers being published today by the eighty or so government-funded small presses ought to remember the literary ancestors who made it possible for them to become authors. And especially Margaret Atwood, who got her start in small press publishing and has worked at every level of the book trade year after year since.

The giant shift of a generation to the other side seems to be part of a general extinction of familiar things. Gone with them are neighbourhood corner stores, family TV, church bells, Monty Python, civility in politics, and one-third of the world's wildlife. Earth is changed. People are frightened. There is a sense of the world's precariousness as crises left over from the twentieth century remain unsolved. For the old especially, the background hum of life is one of distant lamentation. This was the feeling in the air when at the loss of her life partner Graeme Gibson, Atwood began writing miscellaneous pieces that would be published three years later as *Old Babes in the Woods*. I think this collection without knowing it acts out the patterns of a unified literary elegy.

Reviews of the book described it as a mixed bag – a once around the kitchen jumble of tidbits sandwiched between an undeveloped novella about Nel and Tig. Nell is Atwood; Tig is Graeme, and yes, this framing account goes straight to the heart. But I found the in-between speculative fictions compelling as well. They seemed essential to the book as a whole.

For a creative writer who is a public intellectual, grief must be uniquely complicated. How do you find words for a feeling when it's functionally sequestered in your undermind so you can meet a schedule? This must have been the case when Atwood received the Booker, then the Companion of Honour at Buckingham Palace a month after Gibson died. But literature offers a writer models for expressing grief. Atwood tries one out, adapting Tennyson's "Morte d'Arthur" to mourn the death of her cat: "My end draws nigh; 'tis time that I were gone. / Make broad thy cat carrier to receive my weight / And bear me to the vet…" It doesn't sound like Atwood got much solace out of Tennyson. She should have consulted John Milton, poet and public intellectual, and the author of *Lycidas*, an elegy for the death of a college friend.

This poem is a challenge to a reader because it's packed with disparate genres and allusions. Plain-speaking Samuel Johnson condemned it for its artificiality, its unfelt posturing. The poem follows the conventions of the pastoral elegy in order, beginning with the blunt news: Edward King, a promising poet and theologian, drowned in the Irish Sea. Atwood begins with a picture of the *status-quo ante* of Nell and Tig exchanging mirth at their ineptness mastering a First Aid course required of staff on a nature-tour cruise ship. The hard as nails course instructor says: "Drowning is fairly simple. First you need to get the water out."

After blaming fate, the pastoral elegy looks around for sympathy. Milton explores two sources of consolation: classical poetry and the official English Church. The futility of these institutions to give comfort is apparent in a forced sentimentality approaching the ridiculous: "He must not float upon his watery bier / Unwept." That inflated image prompted a young James Joyce, when called upon to offer a statement at a wake for the local pub-keeper's wife whose mortal remains were kept cool in his vat cellar, to blurt out, "She must not float upon his watery beer unwept," before fleeing to his Martello tower pursued by the enraged publican. The middle eight stories in *Old Babes* are like this anecdote – they hang between mock solemnity and the bizarre. Two of the stories seek meaning in the past. Two face the future with an attitude of comic grotesque. Three explore the alternative of aging ungracefully, and Atwood can catch human decay on the page as well as Alice Munro. One story plays with the prospect of an afterlife for individual subjectivity, but this is a stretch. A snail reincarnated as a customer service rep in a bank?

Surviving mates busy themselves with practical things to take their minds off grief; a creative writer deflects it into fanciful artistry. Yet oblique as they seem, the speculative fictions occupying the middle of the collection are doing something. They are recycling a feeling that isn't ready to express itself. Delay is necessary to the process of grieving.

Lycidas resolves on a note of resignation and a return to practicalities, such as gathering the appropriate flowers for the funeral. Atwood's persona Nel closes down the summer home she and Tig restored over the years. The empty house yields the bric-à-brac of marriage – but no answers to the accumulating pressure for meaning which drives the book. Promising a message from beyond, Tig's personal desk box demonstrates only an existential nothingness. This becomes a turning point in the narrator's grief, because Atwood suddenly discards the mask of Nel to speak in her own voice. She speaks of Graeme's father, a Brigadier who liberated part of the Netherlands during World War II. Is there significance for her in his strict division of public and private selves, the one an affable public leader, the other a private poet elegiacally lamenting the bleakness of war and fondling the memory of a secret liaison possibly with a well-known war correspondent? But there's nothing here for her but the implacability of time: "I'm sorry. All I can say is: I hear you. Or I hear something. Or I'm trying to hear something." So much for the past. The life of a family in time offers no meaning to the present.

But time goes on, and Atwood fills it with descriptions written with her customary note of heightened matter-of-factness about her mate regressing in stages into simplicity. They watch the setting sun together ("So sinks the day-star in the ocean bed" – *Lycidas*). "We've had a good run, Graeme says … Thank you." A life shared in time, yet the effort to remember summons a consoling insight: for the bereaved, the dead exist in a "warping or folding of time," as if on the other side of our shadows.

The closing chapter giving its name to the collection is a full-dress short story. It tells of bereft old age in all its formless anxiety and frustration, punctuated by grief-stricken awareness of loss. Yet at another level, writing this book has been one big learning experience, complete with its oscillation between emotional regrouping and tentative exploration. Milton, who used his poetry to teach, engages the conventional movements of the pastoral elegy to give a pattern to grief. For all its artifice, *Lycidas* is full of feeling. It is feeling given form by what physicians and nurses know as the Grief Response Pattern: shock, denial, blame deflection, plea-bargaining, searches for meaning, acceptance – an extended learning experience. I believe Atwood teaches us how to grieve because she first teaches herself. She teaches herself through the process of writing her book.

★ ★ ★

It is the fate of the elderly to exist in a state of loss. Brave soldiers, their mood is one of acceptance of the inevitable. With their place in society gone, they scale down their belongings and ideals. They become one with the legendary Rhygyfarch ap Sulien (died 1099), reputed author of the Welsh myths called *The Mabinogion*, who wrote this lament: "Nothing is of any use to me now, but the power of giving: neither the law, nor learning, nor great fame, nor the deep-resounding glory of nobility, nor honour formerly held, not riches, not wise teachings, not deeds nor arts, not reverence of God, not old age; none of these things retains its station, nor any power." The old remember when they had to say goodbye to their children growing up and becoming their own people. This too is loss. Being at the same time elderly and empty-nested, I need to release myself from the past by a general act of forgiveness. All of it: parents, schools, teachers, authors, politicians. A psychological downsizing so I can be ready for new wonder.

(Courtesy of Digital Sports Photography)

My son's room has now become a storage space, but the chew marks left by his guinea pigs Rosie and Suzie are still there on the bottom edge of the chest of drawers. Going into the bathroom is to be reminded of his growing taller, seen in height measurements penciled on the doorframe and glow-in-the-dark stars stuck to the ceiling. Every few months we find another guitar pick. His mother is happy to discover the Three Musketeers cape of blue satin and silver fleur-de-lys with a scarlet lining. She made it for him, and it will have a use again, along with his small bicycle with the dinosaur patterned tires that he learned to ride on. His exultation when he made his first solo without training wheels, and simply disappeared. Or when he went from house to house delivering newspapers, singing to himself. Now he has his own home, leaving behind his memories.

This also is elegy – the background music of the elderly, and it is with them until their memories leave and go to the other side. *Es war so schön*. It was so beautiful.

Three minutes in Paradise

Seen through the front window – a little girl all dressed up for school with an oversized knapsack on her responsible back. She stops to talk to two ducks. Incredibly, they are wandering down the middle of the street, also well dressed and ungainly. In the sunlight, the drake's head is a blue-green iridescence. A nervous quack from the female. They shuffle out of the way of the schoolgirl who goes on talking anyway, thinking they've turned their backs on her. "I'm sorry, Ducks. I don't have any bread for you." But the ducks aren't interested in being fed by the human girl – they're interested in each other or, to put it accurately, they are in a love daze. For it is the time of year when couples bond, and the ducks are straying from the river so they can dote on each other and look for a place to nest. Reluctantly, the girl proceeds to school, twisting around with her awkward knapsack to have a last glance at the newly married couple who have resumed their command of the street.

To the retiree, watcher-out-of-windows, the little scene offers a glimpse of redemption. What would it be like if you had perceptions like the little girl has all the time? Perceptions that birds can understand her. You would be in a world where things, people, events come true as you imagine them.

The girl is in the realm of Delight which is the meaning of the Hebrew word *Eden*. She talks spontaneously with ducks and presumably other birds and animals. Her open-hearted seeing has been with her since childhood. It is her birthright. It was practised when she slapped the rude table that bumped into her. When she arranged a party for her stuffed animals. What hasn't been with her since childhood and is not in any way her birthright are the stock responses of society, the polite meaningless words that set and re-set a common baseline of narrowed expectation so that everyone can conduct their affairs within the same version of reality.

Her delight promises the enchanted wisdom of Lāo Zi: "From wonder into wonder / Existence opens." It also promises the ridiculous backfiring of intentions that can occur when another person desires something different. This happens to the Raven continually in the Haida myth told by Skaay of Qquuna. The food the Raven wants for his feast is out on a reef. How to get to it? He persuades a Steller's Jay to be the steersman of a canoe. Instead, the Jay shakes and flaps its wings to propel the craft. This doesn't work, so "Then he painted a face on a bracket fungus / and seated it in the stern. 'Look alive there and backpaddle as soon as we come alongside' … the fungus nodded his head." But later when the Raven swears at salmon on the drying rocks because they get caught in his hair, his offended wife says, "'Swim away.' Even the fillets that hung on the drying racks / started to swim."

I want to clear my head of social pieties, and start again with a preternatural sense of adventure. For the child of imagination, the world is populated with living and for the most part congenial presences, an Eden-Earth where "We find ourselves in a buzzing world amid a democracy of fellow creatures."

15
THE DREAM OF HEAVEN

"You were right! There is a heaven after all."

"Ah ... no, not exactly. I wouldn't call it that. But as someone says in an Elizabethan play, 'entertain the proffered fallacy.'"

"Funny that the first person I should meet up here is you. Are you still Northrop Frye?"

"I was, and am, and will be," said the shy angel. He looked down at his bare toes, giving me the opportunity to figure out what he'd said.

He was the same as ever, only taller and thinner, which took away from his impression while on Earth of being a portly gnome. His forehead, which used to resemble a rock sheer, was still forbidding, but his eyes twinkled. While on Earth, he had discovered the recurrent patterns of storytelling in literature. He mapped the human imagination, saving literary criticism from being determined by politics, religion, and psychology.

"Everyone's here. Even that quack Marshall McLuhan. His dream of instantaneous pan-global communication came true.

"He stole the idea from Mallarmé," Frye added in a whisper.

Frye and McLuhan became world celebrities simultaneously in the late Sixties and began to lob shots at each other. I'd arrive late at McLuhan's seminar from a class by Frye to be greeted with "Here comes the small fry." Frye enjoyed teaching; McLuhan didn't, and would schedule his seminar during the rush-hour after a day of writing.

"I can't believe I'm actually here!"

He chuckled. "Don't believe it for a moment. Otherwise it might come true."

"Do I get to meet God?"

"You're looking at him."

"C'mon Norrie. You're not God. Though you did perform a miracle."

"A United Church minister is not qualified to perform miracles."

"What about the precocious student with the crossed eyes? When you asked the class, 'If I were to look for the Kingdom of God, where would I look?' her hand shot up. She always guessed the answer you wanted. 'I'd look in here,' she said solemnly, pointing at her heart. Whereupon you said, 'If you look there, you'll simply continue to be cross-eyed' and watched her fly out of the room in tears."

"The campus gossip story is a type of urban myth."

"A week later, her eyes magically uncrossed. She became a confident, successful student. She credits you for this."

"Evidently, she stopped relying on her intellect and threw away the crutch. But she was never cross-eyed. Exaggeration in the direction of the realistic is typical of stories of this genre."

"About meeting God…?"

"Well, God isn't described in the Bible. Moses got to see his back, which biblical commentators took to mean the physical world."

"Wasn't Jesus God?"

"No. God was Jesus. The distinction is important. However, William Blake said Jesus was the visible form of God. Up here, people are inclined to say 'a' form rather than 'the' form of God. Eternity is nothing if not inclusive."

"Everyone is saved. Hallelujah."

"Are you getting old by any chance? On Earth, I found when I became older that I was more interested in the resurrection of the body than the salvation of the soul."

"But Toronto seems to be resurrected too," I said. "There's the Royal Ontario Museum and beyond it the Park Plaza Hotel."

"What did you expect? An alpine meadow with radiant families gathering daisies?"

"I didn't expect a modern city. In fact, it's mid-town Toronto but without the traffic."

"I got rid of the traffic," Frye said.

I remembered he didn't like cars. He'd been in a car accident on an expressway once. It gave him a broken arm. He trembled all the way to Trent when Gordon Teskey and I drove him up the 401 for a guest lecture. It was January, and on his way to the Guest Suite he saw a mixed group of naked students explode out of the college sauna and throw themselves into the icy river. "Oh, my!" Frye said. That settled him down, but on the drive home he asked me to buy him a bottle of Usher's Green Stripe whiskey.

"We're in Queen's Park. There's your office window."

"It's a logical place for us to meet. The squirrels are a nuisance, however. They want to know your opinion about whether or not the perfect chestnut exists."

"What should I tell them if they ask?"

"In Eternity, everyone strives to be imperfect, provided one doesn't impede someone else's spirit."

"How did you delete the cars?"

"Why not try it yourself? Do you see anything here you don't desire?"

"I don't desire the Rotman Business School. It's out of scale with its surroundings."

"Wish it away."

I closed my eyes and wished the Rotman Business School was on the far side of Lake Ontario, near Rochester, New York.

"That is a distinct improvement," Frye agreed.

"Is that a drone? What's it doing in heaven?"

"It's delivering the campus mail. I'll delete it."

Zap! The drone was gone.

"This is fun. It's like the computer game where you build your own city. Can you add things?"

"Of course. What would you like to add?"

"Small colleges. Like at Oxford."

Suddenly, a row of colleges appeared where the Business School had been on St. George Street.

"Tom Symons will thank you for that. It was his idea. He thought the original colleges were getting too big."

"If Tom's up here, we need to restore the statue of King Edward VII on horseback immediately."

Immediately the statue was back in its place at the top of Queen's Park. The stallion's balls were still painted red by the Queen's Engineers.

"We definitely need more people for the colleges."

The streets became full of students, laughing and chattering.

"I was never comfortable with the CN Tower," Frye said. "It is an allotrope of the Tower of Mammon."

Zap! It was gone.

But cars started to appear again on Queen's Park Crescent. The new AI-controlled all-glass vehicles. Frye hadn't known about them.

Zap! Zap!

"Paradise is a definition in process," Frye pointed out. "Instead of a single providential harmony you have visionaries of every kind creating it."

"I'm remembering your method of teaching. You asked a question, then waited a full half minute for someone to answer."

"Socs never gives his students time to respond. He's too eager to get them to make his point for him. If people are being prompted to locate something in their unconscious, they need to be given time."

"We called it 'the Northrop Frye Pause.' Once you made two parallel lists on the blackboard. You put down 'Body' and 'Blood.' 'Reason and 'Desire.' The colours of 'York' and 'Lancaster' in the War of the Roses. The stripes on the American flag. Then asked: 'What colours come to mind?' Someone with a CCNY accent said, 'Chartreuse and Puce.'"

"Fortunately, Eternity is free of embarrassment and regret."

"If we're in Toronto, there's some people I definitely don't want to run into."

"You'll find you won't need to be forgiven. The sacrifice has already been made."

"So there's a God who forgives!"

Frye made the tiny grimace I remembered whenever he faced a situation where something was plainly obvious to him but not to others. "The reason why we don't see God is because we see through the eyes of God. Emily Dickinson gives him the name *Wonder*."

"Help! I'm trapped inside a Gnostic teaching tale."

"'In my flesh shall I see God.' Do you recall the *Book of Job*?" Frye asked. "It's basically a folk miracle play with one tableau scene and characters delivering monologues."

"I do."

"Job is sitting on a dunghill scratching his boils with the shard of a pot and asking why. Why is this happening to me? What did I do wrong?"

"Atopic dermatitis is common among the elderly," I said stupidly.

"But worse than the boils, Job has to endure the voices of social conformity. They're trying to persuade him that he lives in a fairy tale world where the good are rewarded and the wicked are punished. Job makes a long, beautiful speech in his defence – the dramatic situation of the folk play is that of a trial, and Job wants justice. I've been good. Why am I being punished? Show me the evidence. The superficial answer is that he's probably not done anything wrong except become old and get – what is it? – atopic dermatitis. After all, the Accuser Satan gave him the affliction. Then the voice of God comes out of a whirlwind, and he gives a speech though not as beautiful as Job's. He says "What do you people think you're doing rattling on about a just god rewarding the good and punishing the bad. I am not a just god. I am beyond your moral

Northrop Frye
(Edwin Gailits)

categories and righteousness. Stop projecting that stuff on me. How dare you presume to know who I am? 'Where wast thou when I laid the foundations of the world?' 'Can'st thou draw out Leviathan with an hook?' They look at each other and say, 'Well, no, I guess we can't.' ... You know who Leviathan is, don't you?"

"Leviathan is the world of sin controlled in part by Satan."

"Yes. A society held together by a molecular tension of egos obsessed with the wealth of the material world. Thomas Hobbes wrote a book about it. Then the Almighty begins to extoll his pet dragon, Leviathan. His eyes, his nostrils, his compact scales ... 'I will not conceal his parts,' says God. 'Nor his comely proportions.' He sounds rather proud of his creation. Like any artist, he's admiring his work of art. He uses the word 'Behold.'"

Where is Frye going with this?

"Where do you think Job is at this moment?" Frye asked suddenly.

"I don't know. He's in a trance like me."

"Hmm. That's interesting. Perhaps he is. In any case, he's no longer in the physical world.

"Why not? He's sitting on a dung heap. That's a very physical world."

"Because God is pointing at it. Remember, he said 'Behold.'" That means Job is…"

"Got it! He's in heaven, standing beside God."

"Apparently something happened during God's monologue. Job died. You don't even see it happening."

A Northrop Frye Pause went by. A rush of eternity. Then he said: "It's as if by dying he woke up. Do you think it's possible Job may have been in heaven the whole time?"

"Is there suffering in heaven? Explain the boils."

Frye was becoming ineffable. Like his chapter endings. They would soar up into some unknowable realm of vision as if that's where you'd be if you put his book down and woke up.

"I guess you don't remember the comment I wrote on your Spenser essay?" he said mischievously.

"How can I forget it? You said very nicely that I'd missed the whole point of what I was writing about, which was Edmund Spenser's retelling of the legend of Saint George and the Dragon."

"I reminded you that Saint George is supposed to rescue the parents of his consort, Una. Spenser identifies them as Adam and Eve. They are still in their Garden of Eden, but it is encircled by a dragon."

"Leviathan."

"Yes, though Spenser doesn't name him. Nevertheless, it's the material world. The world of time and space. It encircles human vision, giving us crossed eyes and a general visionary myopia. What do you think will happen when Saint George kills the dragon?"

"There will be no more time and space."

"What will happen when he kills the dragon is that all of space and time will turn inside-out. Now, a space-full, time-full world is at the centre, surrounded by Paradise. Perhaps that's what Saint Paul means by 'the fullness of time'."

I remember now. There was an elusive theme in Frye's writing which made people think he'd lost it and floated off to the moon. Something about the entire body of Nature right out to the Sun, Moon, and Stars contained in the body of the artist. "Paradise can be a pretty big place," I said.

"Of course, in *Genesis*, Eden is the whole Fertile Crescent extending from the Nile to the Indus. Those two rivers are named together with the Tigris and Euphrates. In the last book of the Christian Bible, the same Four Rivers of Eden flow out from beneath the throne of God."

"Are you telling me that right now we're on Earth?"

"It doth require but you awake your faith," Frye quoted seraphically. "Incidentally, I've found that one of the perks of Eternity is that books and plays come to life so you don't have to read them anymore. You don't have to write them either. That certainly ends the agony of finding a publisher."

"Everyone I know is here. My mother. Aunt Alice. Captain Kane. Agneta. Graeme, Bill Blissett too. I want to see them. I don't want to go back. I don't like cars. By the way, how did you do that trick of rearranging reality?"

"We dream in Paradise too. When we need a break from the partying, we wander off and fall asleep guarded by one of Blake's Daughters of Beulah. Occasionally we have a nightmare. The nightmare you're currently having is called 'Life in the Twenty-First Century.' You mistook it for reality. A common error, and easily forgivable."

"From which I woke up here."

"It's better if you don't say *up*. 'The Kingdom of Heaven is all around you,' if you want the more likely translation. Our two dreams must have bumped together, resonated, and begun a dialogue."

"Heaven opens out sideways."

"I have to say, it felt good teaching again. But I must stop slumming. It's time to go and dance with the angels."

Frye dancing with the angels?

"You were having a dream. A dream of heaven."

16
THE DREAM OF FRIENDSHIP

Owen and Natasha's wedding is going to be a celebration of community. There will be doctors and nurses at the beginning of their careers, athletes the couple has run, bicycled, or rowed with, and former resident fellows of Massey College, led by its long-serving former principal, John Fraser. Cousin Andrew Pyper, the bestselling novelist, is coming with his wife Heidi. There's dancing to midnight and a free bar. This is a wedding designed by the young for the young. To my discomfort, it will be entirely secular.

I am to play a role in the proceedings. I will deliver the Toast to the Bride and her Family. Whatever am I going to say at this godless event?

But that is for tonight.

Today is for stealing away with Barbara von Otter, who has come from Sweden for the wedding. We're going to the Toronto Islands. This is something she never did during her teenage years here.

"Didn't your date take you to Ward's Island and accidentally miss the last ferry back?"

"No. And I hope we will return in time for the wedding."

Barbara is anxious as the elderly are about getting lost and arriving late. And she has that tumour at the back of her brain, causing her to see two of me, which must be disorienting.

With the shared fragility of an elderly couple we negotiate a TTC streetcar, the Yonge subway, and another streetcar to the Jack Layton Terminal. The red Toronto streetcars are familiar and reassuring. The high-rise towers are not, but Barbara sees right through them as if they didn't exist. Toronto's ethnographic diversity is new to her and a delight. Everywhere we go, people break into conversation spontaneously, as if divisions of race, gender, class, and age had evaporated. Like many of the European countries that achieved nationhood on the basis of a single ethnicity in the nineteenth century, Sweden doesn't know quite how to relate to its immigrants.

What a great idea to take the Toronto Island ferry! The rumble underfoot as the diesels engage. The shudder of the deck. The wash of the wake against the pilings. Over there to the right is the *Trillium*, an antique ferry used for dance cruises. She has the Edwardian girth to support immense side wheels and a tall black funnel little changed from her launching in 1910. She's a fantasy out of time. And sailboats of the Royal Canadian Junior Yacht Club are dodging our ferry just as they did when I learned to sail in them at age fourteen. We gaze at the receding skyline of the city from the upper deck. Towering buildings sparkle in the August sunlight under fluffy clouds. The city seems to float in the air.

"It is a dream!" Barbara says.

A dream. That is what reality is to the elderly.

We reminisce over a light patio lunch served by a Wards' Island hippie. I speak some Swedish Agneta taught me. Sixty-four years have passed since we first met. It is all coming back. I summon the Barbaras I knew over the years and try to focus them in this elegant woman sitting across from me with time flowing off her shoulders. The thirteen-year-old Branksome Hall schoolgirl in her Scottish kilt. The teenager running away from home and crawling through my bedroom window. The Jarvis Collegiate high-school student writing "Dick Starr" on her history textbook and playing the dating game

Barbara von Otter
Beck Friis

with her best friend Shelley Wild. The sorrowful hug at Shelley's funeral. The day before, we spent a morning catching up on our lives at the café across the river from my house in Peterborough. Being alone with Barbara at restaurants has punctuated our friendship, which makes our lunch on Ward's Island self-conscious. It's probably the last time we'll see each other.

My visiting Sweden had been on Agneta's and my mind through the spring of 1961. But it seemed a faint hope, until at the last moment I discovered the *Bengore Head* was scheduled for a trip to Finland. I signed on in Belfast – I still had my Seaman's Identity Card – and accompanied Captain Stark to the port office to register his cargo manifest. "Overloaded and undermanned, she sailed across the Bay," he reported. A quote from Kipling. The *Bengore Head* was a Baltic lumber carrier given to Britain by Germany as reparation after the war. Head Line sailors favoured a posting to her because the ports she visited were close to home. I favoured her because my grandfather had skippered an earlier *Bengore Head*. And Ted Hayes had just been transferred to her. It promised to be a relaxing late summer voyage.

The first night out we hit a gale. The sea crashed over the bow, slammed against the superstructure, and exploded skyward drenching the bridge lookouts who ducked just in time. The wheelhouse windscreen wipers barely cleared the windows when the next wave broke over the boat. The mast stays sang in the wind. So did I, because I wasn't the least bit frightened: I was exultant. This was truly being at sea. Captain Stark found a headland to shield behind while we rode it out at anchor.

The next day we sailed the Minches, the west coast of Scotland, full of history and desolation. The captain produced a skipping rope and exercised on the outside bridge. We rounded the top of Scotland and sailed through the Pentland Firth to jokes about the ship's inability to overcome the fierce tidal current there – she was a slow steamer. Then across to Copenhagen enjoying a sunny holiday afternoon with the southern shore lined with Danish flags and the northern shore with the flag of Sweden. And sailboats everywhere.

Crossing the Baltic through the night, I settled into the routine of watches. I remember the constant alertness to shipping. But as we neared Leningrad, it seemed another country was celebrating a holiday. Russia had turned out its entire Baltic fleet. We heard the diesel engines over the horizon before we saw the two lines of submarines – menacing, black, stealthy. Captain Stark shook his fist and cursed. Every Head Line captain had bitter memories of the Atlantic War. Those Russian subs were built using captured German blueprints. So were the cruisers which came next, lobbing shells at a target we couldn't make out. The shell splashes showed on the radar screen.

It was a release of tension to enter the Helsinki Archipelago, as beautiful as Canada's Thousand Islands. The aloof Helsinki girls gladly took cigarettes from us, then returned to their conversation. The city businessmen affected English bowler hats and umbrellas that summer. This country wanted to belong to Europe and its defence shield, NATO. I left the *Bengore Head*, carrying a knapsack of canned Guinness and energy bars, and boarded the overnight ferry to Stockholm. European ferries were and always will be party boats, and the centre of the fun was a group of Danish sailors who showed me how to toast with Tuborg. Then Stockholm through brain fog, a low-lying Baltic coastal city with eighteenth-century buildings in the Enlightenment style. Ted Hayes had given me a message to take to a girl he met in Finland.

"Yes, come. Why not?" she said in a bored, indifferent voice.

She was the first of a string of encounters that left me feeling out of my depth and unaware of it. Escorting me back to a main street in Stockholm, she said: "No goodbye kiss. That is only in American movies."

The train journey down the length of southern Sweden was uneventful. Hultrum was a small stop in the countryside with a station master who didn't seem sure of his English. "One mile," he answered when I asked him how far to Stora Hultrum (*stora* means "big," referring to area). I started out jauntily, not knowing that a Swedish *mil* is ten kilometres or 6.2 miles. The barns were all painted red with white trim, with the forest behind them. There were no cars. Night was coming. A French couple responded to my hitchhike request, and delivered me the rest of the way. The manor house seemed strangely quiet. Only one window was lit. An elderly woman opened the door and looked down at me on the step, tar-stained, smelling of Guinness, and totally unexpected. Agneta apparently hadn't reckoned on my coming all this way.

"*Kom i.*"

The elderly woman went to the kitchen and emerged after a while with something that looked like a sandwich on a plate. It was clear she wasn't used to making sandwiches. I sat where she'd put the plate at the end of a long dining-room table. She sat at the far end. The painted otters on the ceiling examined me critically. She tried German. No good. I tried French. This worked a little. The family was returning from Göteborg and she was their grandmother. They would arrive late at night. I might as well go to bed if I was as tired as I looked.

The next morning, I heard children at my bedroom door. They peeked at me and ran away giggling. They were Agneta's first cousins. In the afternoon, sitting on the front steps of the house, the oldest boy tested his high-school English.

"Sean Kane. That is a funny name."

"Why is it funny?"

"It has two sounds. Just Sean Kane."

"Like Pir Gynt?"

"Yes, that is a funny name too."

That was my only confident exchange during the week that followed. I began to sense I was a problem. Not only to the dowager baroness who resembled the Teutonic aristocrat in *Murder on the Orient Express*, but also to Agneta who seemed unsure what to do with me. I watched her from afar as she carried out the senior child's duty of rowing her father along the shoreline while he hauled up crayfish traps. She watched from afar as I rowed her father and uncle along the same shoreline while they blasted Merganser Ducks out of the water with their shotguns, then carried two braces of duck corpses to the house for the womenfolk to praise. Customs I hadn't seen in Canada came to the fore here. They were all connected with social hierarchy. At dinner, the grandmother suddenly put her fork dow. What was wrong? Had she swallowed a shotgun pellet?

"There are thirteen. It is unlucky."

Everybody started counting the number of people at the table. No matter which way they counted, they ended up with me. I was the unlucky thirteenth guest at the Feast of the Gods in Valhalla. An ambiguous Loki who didn't fit with custom. The solution was to separate all the young to eat together on card tables in the kitchen.

The next day, Agneta's mother asked if I'd like to go to Stockholm with them. Barbara would come too.

In Stockholm we watched a pre-Olympic track and field meet between Sweden and Japan. We visited the Canadian ambassador's summer cottage on the archipelago. One night, Barbara's father gave us money and the address of a famous restaurant in a cave in the Old City to have dinner together. We talked small talk. We weren't sure how we were supposed to relate to each other.

Back at Stora Hultrum, I said thank you and goodbye to a kind-hearted Baron von Otter, and boarded the train for the Hook of Holland. I left behind an Agneta speechless with embarrassment, regret, guilt, and helplessness.

A young woman wearing a skimpy top and carrying a water bottle went down the corridor of the train, inviting every interesting-looking person to a party in Copenhagen. Hearty Danes were a relief from socially uptight Swedes, and the party was all drinking and dancing, with people sitting on the floor against the walls. A woman flopped down beside me. It was impossible to guess her nationality because her English was so fluent.

"What did you think of Walter Lippmann's column yesterday?"

"I'm sorry. I don't know who Walter Lippmann is," I said. (He was the distinguished *Washington Post* political columnist who practically invented American foreign policy after the War.)

Copenhagen to Lübeck, then to Rotterdam. During the night, the conductor groped under my pillow for my passport and shined a flashlight on my face. Finally home to Canada where my father's Montreal sales representative stood at the bottom of the gangplank, holding my high school grades at arm's-length like a piece of detritus.

And so we talk about ourselves. Barbara gives me a glimpse of her present life with her partner. He has his own family of children to attend to, grown up and become parents themselves. Then she shows me photos of her former husband. United with him through an arranged marriage, she has suffered one experience of male hierarchy too many. It was she who managed the immense eighteenth-century manor house, who sparkled like a hostess at the parties, who skinned the carcass of the deer he brought home from hunting.

We talk about our generation's ideals and how generous and enduring friendship is. The pleasure of today's wedding is that it is to be a gathering of friends. At its core will be young men Owen trained together with in doubles, quads, and eights on the Otonabee River. For the first event in Bachelor's Week, Dylan, the Best Man, reunited the team that won Gold at the Royal Canadian Henley Regatta a decade before. They repeated the victory, rowing in a category that typically embraces former champions, Olympians, and U.S. college teams competing nostalgically. For the second event in Bachelor's Week, the men gathered at a cottage on Georgian Bay with a week's supply of booze and their racing bikes. Owen crashed and broke his collarbone.

The ferry blows its horn impatiently. Our time here is over.

* * *

Who can describe the magnificence? Baskets of flowers in soft colours hang everywhere. Beneath celestial flower clouds, guests greet each other like long lost angels. There are broad outdoor balconies for people to socialize. A community is celebrating the union of two of its members. That is how the Welsh officiant puts it in his opening remarks:

> *As families and as a community of friends, we have gathered here to witness the marriage of Owen and Natasha and to share in the joy of their mutual love. To this moment they bring the dreams that bind them together. They bring a particular personality and spirit that is uniquely their own, and out of which will grow the reality of their life together. We rejoice in the outward symbol of their inner union, a union created by friendship, respect, and love.*

Friendship. The word keeps coming up. Now it sounds in a faint metaphor from Saint Paul together with the Methodist certainty that every individual has a God-given personality. But there's a pronounced secular emphasis on the freedom of two individuals to shape their own future for themselves, just as they have designed their wedding ceremony. My Toast to the Bride, now trembling inside its clipboard folder, is going to sound the wrong note.

The throng moves in excited chattering groups to the reception hall. And now more flower clouds spread their fragrance over a space big enough for two floor hockey games. And there are more flowers on the tables, with tall white candles burning in glass cylinders. John Fraser is at the next table, surrounded by Massey College alumni. An outspoken monarchist, he is the glorious symbol of the absurdity of living Canada's traditional values in the condition of modernity. I tell John my address to the Bride will make him feel at home.

But the noise in this low-ceilinged room is making my heart race. The young don't talk, they amplify. The most raucous are the athletes; having consumed earlier part of a week's supply of booze brought from Georgian Bay, they cheer each event in the proceedings, injecting an atmosphere of euphoria. The ritual dances are touching. Most moving of all to me is Kel, the mother of the groom, swaying gently in her bare feet with Owen to Kermit the Frog's "Rainbow Connection." Owen with his arm in a sling.

The dinner is punctuated by toasts. The Slavic toasts are historical and sentimental. The Best Man can't finish his list of memories of growing up together with the groom, and dissolves into "I love you Owen" before he breaks into tears. It will be my turn soon. I have to make this toast a success, in spite of my total incapacity for sincerity, especially at weddings.

This is what I said:

The Wedding Toast to Natasha and Owen, August 11, 2023

It's our honour — Kelly's and mine — to propose the Toast to the Bride. I need to warn you that, being academics, we found out what we were supposed to say by researching the custom of the wedding toast back to its origin in aristocratic feudalism. This is going to put a spirit of antiquity in our toast. But why not? Today, let us be aristocrats. We are all lords and ladies of love.

It seems a function of the Toast in ancient times was for the Groom's family to thank the Bride's family for the gift of their daughter ... and her dowry. So, according to tradition, we thank Victor and Lana for the delight of knowing them, and for the gift of Natasha, uniter of families.

A further function of the Toast was to extol the merits of their Groom, thereby reassuring the Bride's family, and probably the Bride herself, that the Groom was a proper match for their daughter, and not a total jerk. In this respect, I can attest that the Groom has been properly educated in the doctrine and discipline of marriage, however antiquated it is. He has a Ph.D. in marriage. All the taxpayers here who have paid for Owen's Social Science and Humanities Research Council scholarships can be reassured that your taxes aren't in vain.

For Owen understands that a marriage is *the fulfillment of social order* ... because it is the fulfillment of the whole *Order of Nature* — of the divine order of the universe — on which the social order is based.

Owen knows this from studying the seventeenth-century poet John Milton, author of *Paradise Lost*. Milton was married three times, so he found the secret to a good marriage the hard way. A good marriage, he says, is an *ongoing conversation between two civilized adults*. To illustrate this, he pictures the first married couple, Adam and Eve, exchanging long, eloquent speeches with each other in Paradise ... while entirely naked. They didn't have a fig leaf between them. (This was marriage before the Fall. After the Fall, they lost their eloquence. They mumbled and sulked.)

Natasha and Owen first met in Balzac's café on Princess Street in Kingston, and they immediately began to talk. They talked and talked ... and by all accounts they haven't stopped talking since.

The wedding website is cryptic about how they spent that first night... I like to think of the poet William Blake and his beloved Catherine reading the Adam and Eve scene in *Paradise Lost* out loud to each other in their back garden in London ... completely naked. Recapturing the innocent eloquence of wedded bliss, Blake understood what Milton meant by the "conversation" which is a good marriage.

Further evidence of Owen's education in marriage: he has published two scholarly papers on a near contemporary of Shakespeare by the name of Edmund Spenser (1552–1599). Spenser is unique among poets because while everybody else wrote love sonnets to an unobtainable ideal lady, or to a coy mistress, or to a Beautiful Youth in Shakespeare's case, Spenser wrote love sonnets ... TO HIS WIFE!

He wrote eighty-eight love sonnets to Eliza.

For the wedding day, he presented her with a wedding ode, a poem with a refrain meant to be sung... It was, you could say, his Toast to the Bride.

You see, Lady Eliza is the daughter of the Earl of Cork, so Spenser's main objective is to demonstrate to her parents that their daughter's marriage to him is the fulfillment of the Order of Nature ... itself the fulfillment of the Order of the Universe.

This he demonstrates by giving his wedding song 365 lines, twenty-four stanzas, and a refrain that alters in relation to the number of hours of darkness and daylight on that one day of the year, in the Northern Hemisphere, at that one longitude and latitude, in southern Ireland.

Meanwhile taking into account the variance between a solar year and a sidereal year – that is, a year measured by the fixed stars, such as the constellations of the Zodiac. (Owen will be glad to explain these intricacies to you in detail later if you stop him between dances.)

Is the marriage of Owen and Natasha, today, the fulfillment of a divine order?

We knew little about Natasha in the months after their meeting, except that she was training to be a doctor.

For us, this was sufficient evidence of a divine order.

She liked climbing the back slopes of mountains, which suggested she was sure-footed and aspiring ... a mountain goat.

No sign of natural order here ... but possibly the desire for one.

Then it became time for her birthday. It turned out Natasha was born on January 9. Which makes her a Capricorn. A goat in the Zodiac. Capricorns are said to be all about ambition, endurance, memory, a reborn Golden Age.

(Owen, if you're interested, is a Libra ... unlike his Best Man, whose birthday is a day later – actually a day and a year later: Libras are proportion, balance, diplomacy, justice.)

But back to the signs of the Zodiac – which is all that's left in our time of a once popular belief in an Order of Nature.

January 9, the day of Natasha's birth ... believe it or not ... is also *my* birthday! ... The ninth of January. Many years earlier.

There! Have I not persuaded you that there is a Divine Order?

This is a marriage made in heaven.

The stars are here with us tonight...

So in the spirit of antiquity, let me pronounce our words, Kel's and mine, for the toast.

These words...

To Natasha and Owen...

May the universe surround you!

May angels dance around you!

May love astound you!

And children play at your feet!

My Lords and Ladies, let us salute their future: to Natasha and Owen...

★ ★ ★

The response was more than polite. For the rest of the evening, people taking a break from the dancing came up and introduced themselves, curious to meet Owen's weird parents. The athletes simply bumped knuckles. The speech had touched a chord.

Milton's Adam and Eve seem like new-born friends in an arrested moment of wonder. But I can't recall if Milton had much to say about friendship. Spenser did though. He places Friendship side-by-side with Love in his epic panorama of ideal ethical behaviour. Friendship is a secular virtue belonging to the Elfs. Love is a spiritual virtue in Humans. The two races join together at a triumphant wedding of the elfin hero and human heroine who first met in a country of Friendship.

Andrew Pyper, Heidi Pyper, Barbara von Otter

I wonder if Friendship is the governing ethic of today's young. This spontaneous, unscripted openness to another person that crosses boundaries of age, class, race, and gender. Diffuse, amiable, it pops up everywhere. The restaurant server who assumes an informal kinship. The Ohio tourist at the ferry dock who asks if Canadians are unfriendly to Americans. The TTC official who gives careful directions. The Roman brotherhood between Owen and his Best Man. Friendship was a value Barbara and my hierarchy-dissolving generation struggled to define in small private ways. Once out in the open in an egalitarian society, friendship was free to unfold its dimensions, from the readiness to be helpful to a stranger, to what the Bible calls "loving kindness" – looking out for and taking care of one another.

Yes, the wedding was a joining of love and friendship. I wanted to add the hope that love and friendship are also a force of attraction in the cosmos. They hold the world together.

NOTES

Copyright page

The disclaimer, "The names in this book are real, the characters fictitious," is borrowed from *As I Was Going Down Sackville Street: A Phantasy in Fact* (1937) by Oliver St. John Gogarty. Instead of writing a factual autobiography, Gogarty brought early twentieth-century literary Dublin to life in recreated conversations, yarns, anecdotes, gossip and satire – forms that invite exaggeration and cartoon. I'm sure the origin of his literary style is the Irish pub. Other writers from the Celtic Renaissance period found this lightly fictionalized memoir form congenial, most notably Ella Young in *Flowering Dusk* (1945).

1. Canada's National Publisher

Hugh Kane's love of New York dates from the mid-1930s when he stayed with his Uncle Tom then at the height of his career as a Shakespearean character actor with occasional roles in film. Whitford Kane (1881–1956), next door neighbour to Orson Welles and mentor to Katharine Hepburn, enjoyed the affection of Irish-American audiences, rewarding them with a benignity that filled the theatre. I have a ten-year-old's memory of visiting him in his basement apartment in a brownstone just north of Greenwich Village, to be examined by cats lodged in floor-to-ceiling bookcases. Uncle Tom's partner and Hugh's lifelong friend was the film star Hiram Sherman (1908–1989).

Hugh served in Holland and Germany with the Royal Canadian

Artillery. Jack commanded a motor torpedo boat on the North Sea. I am using James King's *Jack: A Life with Writers* (Knopf 1995), supplemented by Ruth Panofsky's *The Literary Legacy of the Macmillan Company of Canada* (University of Toronto Press 2012) for Hugh. Roy MacSkimming's *The Perilous Trade: Publishing Canada's Writers, 1946–2006* (McClelland & Stewart 2007) is a business history of the major English-language publishing firms.

Briefly a mother

In the last decade of her life, Alice Kane gave me a handwritten bound volume of memories of her childhood and mine every Christmas. The rhyme chanted by mother and child is by W. H. Davies (1871–1940), a popular poet in his time.

2. The Hero

The mission statement about building character is in *Past and Present* issued by Crescent School (Summer 2015): 16, augmented by Aristotle's *Nicomachean Ethics* 4.3 and Cicero's *On Duties* 1.43.152, *Tusculan Disputations* 3.7, and *On Invention* 2.54.163–5. The "ancient reluctant conscript" is a speaker in Carl Sandburg's poem "Old Timers." C.S. Lewis's quote is from *The Magician's Nephew* (1955; Scholastic 1995): 8. For *The Prospectus of Crescent School* (n.d.), see pp. 7, 15.

Who will speak for wonder?

The last commercial fling with wonder occurred in 2017–2018. The story of "Ivon Tortik" is in Alice Kane's *The Dreamer Awakes*, with an introduction by Robert Bringhurst, edited by Sean Kane (Broadview Press 1995): 21–29.

3. Wonder

Alice Kane recalled her posting to the Parkdale branch of the TPL in an audio recording titled *Children's Librarianship: The Early Days* (unpublished). Her definition of the wondertale can be found in her *The Dreamer Awakes* 169. She spoke about letting a story tell itself in Heather Kirk "River without End. Stories without End," CM Archive 19: 6 (November 1991) online <https://www.cmreviews.ca/cm/cmarchive/vol19no6/alicekane.html>. Whitehead is describing the power of the artist in *Dialogues of Alfred North Whitehead*, recorded by Lucien Price (Mentor 1954): 104.

4. The Open Road

I quote the opening of "McAndrew's Hymn" from Rudyard Kipling *Selected Poems* (2004): 72, 69. This Folio Edition originally belonged to Robertson Davies. The *Manual of Seamanship, Volume 1*, the Admiralty charts, and the *Ship Captain's Medical Guide* originally belonged to my grandfather. The now forgotten parodist is James Kenneth Stephen (1859–1892).

5. First Love

The two girls in silk kimonos are in Yeats's "In Memory of Eva Gore-Booth and Con Markievicz" from *The Collected Poems of W.B. Yeats*, 2nd rev. ed. (New York: Scribner 1996): 235. The phrase "the world's longest undefended border" is used sexually in George Jonas's "American Girl: A Canadian View" in Al Purdy ed. *The New Romans: Candid Canadian Opinions of the U.S.* (Hurtig 1968): 5.

"Young Love, First Love" was written by Ric Cartey and Carole Joyner in 1956. Sonny James's recording of the song reached number one on the *Billboard* composite list of the top 100 songs from all pop genres in 1957.

6. Becoming a Writer

Gibson described his time in Edinburgh, London, and Oaxaca in his Writers' Trust of Canada Margaret Laurence Lecture of June 28, 2011: 5. Eugene Benson described his editing of *Five Legs* in his *The Symmetry of the Tyger: A Memoir* (Rock's Mills Press 2019): 127, identifying the deceased Western student as Wally Ryerson. I'm quoting a copy of the editorial letter Benson sent to Gibson in September of 1960 and the reply Benson received back, which he gave to me on January 12, 2022. James Joyce puts his remark about genius into the mouth of Stephen Dedalus in the Scylla and Charybdis chapter of *Ulysses*, where it sounds more pompous than my paraphrase. Richard Fariña's "Children of Darkness" was written in 1965 and recorded by Joan Baez and Mimi Fariña. Bob Rodger's novel is *The Devil's Party: Who Killed the Sixties?* (Friesen Press 2015). Graeme commented about being edited by Dennis Lee in his reminiscence, "Kind Of Squash" in Karen Mulhallen, Donna Bennett, and Russell Brown, ed. *Tasks of Passion: Dennis Lee at Mid-Career* (Descant 1982): 16–17.

An original form of this chapter was published in *Remembering Graeme*, a booklet produced for members of the Writers Union of Canada in 2020.

A sacred trust

Blake's inspirational stanza serves as the preface to his epic *Milton* (1810). Northrop Frye joked about the elevated status of the accountant in Canada often in his lectures. In 2004, CBC-TV broadcast a series on Great Canadians which was seen by one million viewers. Tommy Douglas was named "Greatest Canadian" in an online vote when the contest was over.

Literary studies today

See George Grant "The University Curriculum" in Howie Adelman and Dennis Lee, ed. *The University Game* (Anansi 1968): 55, 61–62.

8. *The Liberal Arts College*

Gordon Teskey's reminiscence is in his *Spenserian Moments* (Harvard University Press 2019): 22–3. Ian McLachlan's *The Seventh Hexagram* was published in 1976. His *Helen in Exile* was published by Dial Press in New York and Macmillan in London and Toronto in 1980.

Professor John Wadland, newly appointed to Canadian Studies and the *To Know Ourselves* project, first advocated interdisciplinarity to a cautious Tom Symons, persuading him by means of a circular to consultants, including George Grant who replied curtly, "It's all right, I guess." The interdisciplinary programs distinguishing Trent throughout the '70s and '80s included the first department of Cultural Studies in North America.

It's revealing to see how much Tom Symons and Vincent Massey (1887–1967) had in common. Massey attended Balliol College, Oxford; Symons attended Oriel, Oxford – two colleges with a pronounced British Commonwealth orientation. Returning to Canada, Massey joined the University of Toronto as a lecturer in history; so did Symons, though he wasn't in a position to supervise the donation of his family's wealth to the University as Massey did with Hart House, Burwash Hall, and Massey College, a residential community for graduate students. Symons was dean of Devonshire House, a residence for students in the professional faculties next door to Massey College. He was involved in university planning at the highest level, serving with Northrop Frye and Marshall McLuhan on an advisory committee to university president Claude Bissell.

Both men became policy advisors to federal party leaders. Massey was a brains trust and political operative for Mackenzie King before his 1925 Liberal election sweep. King rewarded him with the headship of the Canadian High Commission in London, a posting Massey regarded as equivalent to an ambassadorship, much to King's disgust. Massey was close to the royal family due to social ties with the English aristocracy nurtured since his days at Balliol. Symons, who must have aspired to the prized London posting, settled for head of the Commonwealth Universities Institute and regular tea with the Queen Mother and the future King Charles.

Vincent Massey returned to Canada with some reluctance and turned down political office (as did Symons). He chaired the Royal Commission on National Development of the Arts, Letters, and Sciences (to give its full name and mission), which secured funding for various federal agencies like the National Film Board and the National Research Council. The Massey Report led to the creation of the Social Sciences and Humanities Research Council and the Canada Council. It called for support to Canadian culture "to help our nation express itself." Two decades later, Symons chaired a commission that revealed the foreign domination of research interests and hirings at Canada's universities. As the Massey Report Canadianized the arts, the Symons Report Canadianized the universities.

Following another Canadian social pattern, neither the Masseys nor the Symons-Bulls were long settled Old Canadian families: they were Methodist farmers. Both Vincent Massey and Tom Symons had younger brothers in the creative arts, both had two sons, both had canny wives.

For all its coincidences I don't mean to press this pairing closely. It is nothing more than the career path of the twentieth-century upper-class colonial gentleman. But Massey and Symons differ strongly in personality: by all accounts, Massey was an irritating elitist and class snob. Tom wasn't, because he was educated by his creations, particularly Trent and its Peter Robinson College which changed before his eyes from a feudal community into an experiment in egalitarian education. Also, Tom, unlike Massey, was a teacher at heart and passionate about the study of Canada.

I published the first part of this chapter as "Trent in High Autumn" in *Trent* 53: 1 (Fall 2022): alumni news <mycommunity.trentu.ca/trentnews150>; and the last part as "The CanLit Children of Trent" in *Trent* 53: 2 (Spring 2023): 23–26.

9. A National Literature

My *Deep Ecology Poetics* was finally written in 2025, but is not yet published. The lines by Hölderlin (1770–1843) are from his "As, when on festive days," translated by Christopher Middleton who also characterizes the "fields of vision crossed by whirlwinds of fire." I am quoting Friedrich Hölderlin Eduard Mörke *The Selected Poems* (1972): xxii. Alice Munro's "The Time of Death," originally published in *Canadian Forum* (1956), can be found in *Canadian Short Stories*, edited by Robert Weaver as an Oxford World Classic in 1960, reprinted with an introduction by William Toye and afterword by David Stover in 2008. Lee described a Canadian voice in poetry in his seminal "Cadence, Country, Silence" published in *Liberté* 14: 6 (1972): 65–88 and *Open Letter* 2:6 (Fall 1973): 34–53. I write about Lee's concern with Voice in "The Poet a Shepherd of Being" in *Tasks of Passion* 121-142. For John Moss, see *The Paradox of Meaning* (Turnstone Press 1999): 235. The best explanation of the Canadian Red Tory is by the political scientist Gad Horowitz in his famous essay "Conservatism, Liberalism and Socialism in Canada: An Interpretation," *Canadian Journal of Economics and Political Science* 32 (1966): 143–171. Ian McLachlan's observation was made during a Trent English Department discussion of the new CanLit in 1973. The Heidegger quotation is from "What Are Poets For?" (1946) in Martin Heidegger *Poetry, Language, Thought* (Harper 2011): 89–139. For Lee's definitive elegy, see *The Death of Harold Ladoo* in his *Heart*

Residence (Anansi 2017): 85–104. Robert Bringhurst first published the poem in his Kanchenjunga Press Chapbook # 1 in 1976.

On Hugh Kane's suggestion Lee's *Alligator Pie* was divided from the nonsense verse for older children which was published simultaneously in 1974 as *Nicholas Knock, and Other People*. Doug Gibson remembers that Kane decided the first volume should be called *Alligator Pie*. See "Publishing in Canada: Interview with Douglas Gibson" in *Scottish Books International* online August 16, 2021 <https://scottishbooksinternational.org/publishing-in-canada-interview-with-douglas-gibson/> He recalls that in 1974 "there were no children's bookstores and only one children's publisher" in Canada. When he arrived at Macmillan that year, "the corridors were alive with gossip of how [Hugh Kane] was championing a crazy project, a couple of children's books by a poet named Dennis Lee that would need to sell ten times the usual number of copies sold by Canadian children's books before they broke even. The whole thing was going to be a disaster." <https://49thshelf.com/Blog/2012/06/07/Dennis-Lee-s-Groundbreaking-Alligator-Pie-is-Reborn>

My guess is that the author of "Alligator Kahlua" is Ian McLachlan.

10. *Prophet to a Nation*

Symons wrote about the editing session in "Generalissimo Lee" in *Tasks of Passion* 25–28. "Yet still they take the world full force on their nerve ends" concludes the 4th *Civil Elegy* of 1972 as published in *Heart Residence* 39. The statement "we have inverted Heaven and Hell" is in *Place d'Armes* (McClelland & Stewart 1967): 212. Lee's "negative catalyst going through life on autopilot" is quoted in Ian Young "A Whiff of the Monster" in *Canadian Notes and Queries* 77 (Summer/Fall 2009).

Immediately after the dinner party embarrassment, Findley

wrote a long apologetic letter to Atwood and Gibson, explaining that Symons had diabolically tempted him with the option of the suicide that awaits a failed writer, which put him into a drunken depression. Confirmed by Bill Whitehead, this is the official account of the event in Sherrill Grace's *Tiff: A Life of Timothy Findley* (Wilfrid Laurier Press 2020): 221–223. She doesn't mention the events of the night before because Findley left them out of the account. Symons' unpublished novel is *The Water Walker*. His description of the archetypal Canadian married couple is excerpted in *Dear Reader: Selected Scott Symons*, edited by Christopher Elson (Gutter Press 1998): 255–271.

What's to be done with the past?

I am quoting Yeats's "Are You Content?" in the *Collected Poems* 321.

11. The Critical Essay

William Blissett's *The Porpoise and the Otter* (Rock's Mills Press 2022) was reviewed by Min Wild in *TLS* (6 October 2023): 24. Montaigne's statements are from *The Complete Collected Essays of Montaigne*, translated by Donald M. Frame (Stanford University Press 1958).

In regard to the health of the public discourse in a liberal democracy, an Abacus poll done between December 7–12, 2023 found only one in ten people were taught how to discuss controversial social and political issues in school. Fifty percent of teachers in another recent poll said they lacked adequate training in civic education. Abacus found that people who hadn't been taught "how democratic institutions and government work" are less likely to vote ("A civil Canadian society needs solid civic education." Cited in an editorial in *The Globe and Mail*, on January 27, 2024 <theglobeandmail.com/opinion/editorials/article-a-civil-canadian-society-needs-solid-civic-education/>).

12. Survival

Jack McClelland's "We are a Canadian firm" is quoted in James King's *Jack: A Life with Writers* 220. See 164–170 for the earliest attempts to secure corporate loans. I contrast Mowat's brief academic foray with the reactions of other poets and scholars returning from war to the University of Toronto in *Inward of Poetry* (Porcupine's Quill 2011): 17–22. Mowat's memoir of the Hastings and Prince Edward Regiment veterans can be found along with other personally meaningful life events in his *Eastern Passage* (McClelland & Stewart 2011): 115–151. Hugh Kane's observation about undercapitalized expansion is in *Jack* 162 n 5 together with the final attempts at business and government support: 192–193. For Pierre Berton's prominence at M&S, see 124–125, 148, 211–212.

13. Mastery

Geoffrey Hinton's prediction is in *The Guardian* (December 27, 2024): <https://www.theguardian.com/technology/2024/dec/27/godfather-of-ai-raises-odds-of-the-technology-wiping-out-humanity-over-next-30-years> George Grant on the "mastery of chance" in "The University Curriculum" 47 is quoting Jacques Ellul's *The Technological Society* (1954; Vintage 1965): xxxiii. "The Prayer" was written in 1998 by David Foster, Carole Bayer Sager, Tony Renis, and Alberto Testa for Céline Dion and Andrea Bocelli.

14. Dying

Frye's accounts of perspective in Canadian art are in his *The Bush Garden: Essays on the Canadian Imagination* (Anansi 1971): for West Wind," see "Canadian and Colonial Painting" (1940): 201; for "deeper into the forest," see "Conclusion to a *Literary History of Canada*" (1965): 223–225. "New Year's Poem," first published in

Avison's *Winter Sun* (1960), is reprinted in *Always Now: The Collected Poems*, 3 volumes (Porcupine's Quill 2003). Regarding the elite community of Canadian writing activists, we are inclined to forget that Canada was a largely white country until the Immigration Act of 1976. "Canadians of European origin still accounted for 96 percent of the 21.5 million people in the total population" in 1971. That year, "There were only 35,000 Canadians who identified as African or Black in the census, a number that would grow to 250,000 by 1991. Similarly, the population of those who identified as Asian grew from just 121,000 in 1971 to 1.6 million in 1991." From Ed Broadbent, Frances Abele, Jonathan Sas, and Luke Savage *Seeking Social Democracy: Seven Decades in the Fight for Equality* (ECW 2023): 71. Sadly, Malcolm Ross's *The Impossible Sum of Our Traditions* received little play following its publication by McClelland & Stewart in 1986. For the term "decolonization," see Eugene Benson *The Symmetry of the Tyger* 228.

"Morte de Smudgie" (Atwood's cat) is in her *Old Babes in the Woods* (McClelland & Stewart 2023): 42. "Drowning is fairly simple" 3. Joyce's pun on "bier"/"beer" in *Lycidas* is told by Oliver St. John Gogarty (a.k.a. "Buck Mulligan") in his *It Isn't This Time of Year at All: An Unpremeditated Autobiography* (London: MacGibbon & Kee 1954): 76. "All I can say is: I hear you" is in Atwood 210. The "folding of time" 214. The idea of a metaphysical wormhole for departed spirits may have been suggested by Hilary Mantel's *A Memoir of My Former Self* 99 which Atwood praised in a jacket quote. Rhygyfarc ap Sulien's lament is in MS *Cotton Faustina* CI, Part II, fols 66–94. *Es war so schön* is at the end of Goethe's *Faust*.

Three minutes in Paradise

I'm quoting the last line of the 1st Analect from an edition of Lāo Zi that was popular in my generation: *The Way of Life according to Lao Tzu*, translated by Witter Bynner (Putnam 1944): 25. I am quoting

Robert Bringhurst's monumental translation of the Haida oral philosopher Skaay of Qquuna in *Being within Being* (Douglas & McIntyre 2001): 336–337. The phrase "democracy of fellow creatures" belongs to A.N. Whitehead in *Process and Reality* (1929; New York: The Free Press 1978): 50.

15. *Heaven*

In *Northrop Frye: A Biography* (Random House 1989): 215. John Ayre tells the correct version of the event that gave birth to the campus myth. For the entire body of nature contained in the imagination, see Frye's *Fearful Symmetry: A Study of William Blake* (Princeton University Press 1947): 267–268.

16. *Friendship*

Captain Stark's "Overloaded and undermanned" is from Kipling's "The Ballad of Bolivar." Andrew Pyper, the most technically skilled writer of fiction in Canada, died on January 3, 2025, at the age of fifty-six.

ABOUT THE AUTHOR

Sean Kane began his academic career at the University of Toronto. Following an appointment to the Department of English there, he joined Trent University, becoming the founding chair of Cultural Studies. His now classic *Wisdom of the Mythtellers* established the political ecology of myth as the popular alternative to twentieth-century approaches through psychology. Besides scholarly publications, he is the author of *Virtual Freedom*, a campus novel, and *Raccoon: A Wondertale*, with Afterword by Margaret Atwood.

He lives on the Otonabee River in Peterborough, Ontario, downstream from Trent University where he is emeritus professor.

IMAGE CREDITS

The author and publisher gratefully acknowledge the following copyright holders and owners for their kind permission to reproduce the images included in this book. Page 5: Hugh Kane Archives. 7: Anne McClelland/McMaster University. 8: Hugh Kane Archives. 11: Sean Kane. 20: From Sean Kane's copy of *The Prospectus of Crescent School* (n.d., probably 1933), p. 15. 21: As above, p. 29. 31: Sean Kane. 34: Sean Kane. 42: Sean Kane. 44: Sean Kane. 45: Toronto Public Library Archives, object number TPL-A-0328. 58: Sean Kane. 60: Sean Kane. 61: Sean Kane. 62: Sean Kane. 71: Sean Kane. 79: Barbara Beck-Friis. 83: Barbara Beck-Friis. 100: Harold Barkley, *Toronto Star*/Getty. 102: Sean Kane. 103: Sean Kane. 104: Sean Kane. 107: Duncan Cameron/Library and Archives Canada/C-036222. 112: Sean Kane. 121: Trent University. 126: Trent University. 127: Trent University. 129: Sean Kane. 138: John D. Harbron fonds/Library and Archives Canada/PA-207193. 144: Sean Kane. 146: Sean Kane. 153: Sean Kane. 156: Sean Kane. 160: Agence Opale/Alamy. 167: Rock's Mills Press. 179: Claire Mowat. 185: Sean Kane. 186: Sean Kane. 199: Andrew Johnston. 203: Google Arts & Culture asset ID: 1AHpJ6VRUB1RVQ. 210 (both): Sean Kane. 211: Digital Sports Photography, Thorold, Ontario. 219: Edwin Gailits. 224: Barbara Beck-Friis. 231: Sean Kane. 235: Sean Kane. 249: Sean Kane.

www.ingramcontent.com/pod-product-compliance
Lightning Source LLC
Chambersburg PA
CBHW071234070526
44583CB00017B/2170